1988

From the Rising of the Sun

American University Studies

Series IX

History

Vol. 20

PETER LANG

New York · Berne · Frankfurt am Main · Paris

Brandon H. Beck

FROM THE RISING OF THE SUN

English Images of the Ottoman Empire to 1715

PETER LANG

New York · Berne · Frankfurt am Main · Paris

Library of Congress Cataloging-in-Publication Data

Beck, Brandon H.
  From the Rising of the Sun.

  (American University Studies. Series IX,
History; vol. 20)
    Bibliography: p.
    Includes index.
    1. Turkey – Foreign opinion, British.   2. Public opinion – Great Britain.
  3. Turkey – History – 1453 – 1853.   4. Turkey – History – 1683 – 1829.
  I. Title.   II. Ottoman Empire.   III. Series.
  DR479.G7B43   1987   956.1'01   86-20943
  ISBN 0-8204-0350-4
  ISSN 0740-0462

CIP-Kurztitelaufnahme der Deutschen Bibliothek

Beck, Brandon H.:
From the Rising of the Sun : Engl. Images of the
Ottoman Empire to 1715 / Brandon H. Beck. – New
York ; Berne ; Frankfurt am Main : Lang, 1987.
  (American University Studies : Ser. 9,
  History ; Vol. 20)
  ISBN 0-8204-0350-4

NE: American University Studies / 09

© Peter Lang Publishing, Inc., New York 1987

Printed by Weihert-Druck GmbH, Darmstadt (West Germany)

To my Parents

Contents

Preface

Western civilization has long been characterized by its interest in the wider world. In sixteenth-century England that interest embraced the newest world, America; the most familiar world, Europe; and, to the east, and very near, the world of the Ottoman Turks. In 1603 an English historian cited America as the only part of the world still untouched by Ottoman power, and considered her more fortunate in that than in her rich mines. Readers in continental Europe and in England were interested in the Turks; on the European side a vast and varied literature existed from the fifteenth century on. Significant examples appeared in English translation. Beginning at the end of the sixteenth century, English writers began to construct their own literary edifice. This book is a study of that writing.

Early writers on the Ottoman Empire were utterly confident that they understood their subject. Many visited Istanbul, and wrote first-hand accounts. Yet they were handicapped by many preconceptions, and found it difficult to form new ones: *Coelum non animum mutant, qui trans mare currunt* ("Those who cross the sea change their sky, not their attitude"—Horace). Today's traveller to Turkey can be concerned only with the history of Ottoman expansion into Europe rather than with the threat of it; his view of Islam may be less parochial than that of earlier travellers; he may speak Turkish, as they did not, and he will be among the Turkish people to a far greater extent than was possible earlier. He will encounter personal friendliness and warmth rarely reported in the earlier writings. But he can hardly step down on the platform at Sirkeci Station, or sail into the Bosporus, or even alight from his plane at Yeşilköy Airport without some of the images from the early writing in mind. This book will attempt to explore the development and durability of these images, to relate Ottoman and European histories to each other, and to shorten twentieth-century distances still further.

*****

The transliteration of names follows modern Turkish, while excerpts from English works generally retain the original spelling.

Among my mentors, I owe special thanks to Professor Oron J. Hale, University of Virginia; Professor Stanford J. Shaw of the University of California at Los Angeles; Professor George Huppert and Professor John B. Wolf of the University of Illinois at Chicago Circle; Professor Dean Miller and, most of all, Professor Perez Zagorin of the University of Rochester. Ms. Sonia Anderson gave me useful information. The holdings of the Newberry Library in Chicago and the Folger Shakespeare Library in Washington were essential to my work.

Joseph Forte, of the Phillips County Community College Library in Helena, Arkansas, and Rosemary Green of the Howe Library of Shenandoah College in Winchester, Virginia were of great help. Mrs. Roma Richardson of Phillips College skillfully typed from my manuscripts.

Mr. C. Kamil Müren, Director of the Office of Culture and Information at the Turkish Consulate, and Mr. Cem Tarhan, Counselor at the Turkish Embassy, kindly provided me with a wide choice of pictures for the frontispiece of this book.

My wife, Patricia McGrath Beck and son, Brian, have been understanding and helpful through several summers of work.

November 22, 1985   B. H. B.

Introduction

The Ottoman Sultan Süleyman I, the Magnificent, died in 1566, leading his army in Hungary. His death ended the tenth consecutive successful reign in Ottoman history. Ten rulers whose reigns spanned 250 years had conquered large parts of three continents. In Europe, the Ottomans were on the Danube and beyond; Süleyman had besieged Vienna in 1529, and an Ottoman army would attack the city again in 1683. The Ottomans were a dreadful menace to Europe for four centuries.

Who were the Ottomans? The name derived from the Turkish *Osmanli*, or followers of Osman (1280-1324). Osman was the founder of a small but powerful principality in northwestern Anatolia that became the Ottoman Empire. By the sixteenth century, the name "Ottoman" was associated both with Osman's dynastic heirs and with the highly organized military and ruling class that served the dynasty. The imperial city, and seat of the dynasty after 1453, was Istanbul, the former Constantinople. For Ottomans, Istanbul was much like "a small town, where everyone knew and was known by everyone."[1] The city was open to European visitors, but they remained aliens, facing a towered and guarded wall of Ottoman greatness and pride, difficult to scale or to see beyond. There were European voices from beyond the wall, from within the Sultan's residence and seat of government, Topkapi Saray, but the accounts of Europeans in the Sultan's service remain shadowy, limited in scope, and taken far too readily as definitive accounts of Ottoman realities.[2] Europeans who merely visited Istanbul were more numerous, but they too faced serious handicaps in trying to describe these Ottoman realities. Nevertheless, their descrip-

1

tions were met throughout Europe with great interest. This was nowhere more true than in Elizabethan and Stuart England. For England, the military threat was not imminent. Between England and the "cruell and horrible Pagans stands the Germaine nation as the Bullwark of Christendome," wrote an Elizabethan author in 1595.[3] Yet even by that time distances were shortening. Commercial relations between England and the Ottoman Empire began in the 1580's, while English writers began to construct a great literary edifice. Their works superseded the older "Englished" works of Continental writers. English works on the Ottomans offered a panorama of colorful, vivid, and lasting images of an otherwise unutterably strange part of the world. In an account written originally at the end of the Elizabethan era and printed throughout the seventeenth century, Richard Knolles described the Ottoman Empire as a power without limits:

> ... there is in this world nothing more admirable and strange; of the greatness and lustre thereof, nothing but the beauty of itself, and drunk with the wine of perpetual Felicity, holdeth all of the rest of the world in scorn, thundering out nothing ... but Bloud and War, with a Full persuasion in time to rule over all, prefixing unto itself no other limits than the uttermost bounds of the earth from the rising of the Sun to the setting of the same.[4]

In Knolles' Empire it was part of the coronation of Sultan Mehmet III (1595-1603) for the Sultan to be designated

> Emperour of the Turks and lord of all, from the rising of the Sun unto the going down of the same.[5]

The Ottomans' grasp fell short only of America, "not more fortunate with her rich mines than in that she is also farre from so great and dangerous an enemy."[6]

Richard Knolles never visited the Levant, but Byron said that Knolles' writing made him want to do so. John Evelyn, who also never visited Turkey, saw Turkish warhorses taken at Vienna in

1683 displayed in St. James' Park, and could readily imagine the Turkish host:

> . . . the furniture, consisting of embroidery on the saddle, housings, quiver, bow, arrows, scymeter, sword, mace, of battle-axe *à la Turcisq.* . . . One may estimate how gallantly and magnificently these infidels appear in the field, for nothing could be more glorious.[7]

The first chapter that follows surveys the world of war, diplomacy, and commerce that was the nexus between the Ottoman Empire and Europe. The second surveys the earliest images that contact evoked, concentrating on those works which appeared in English. The following chapters examine the establishment of the English presence in the Ottoman Empire, and then English writing itself down to the early eighteenth century.

1

The World of Islam and the World of War

Christian Europeans and Muslim Turks met as enemies, and remained so. In the tenth and eleventh centuries European Crusaders fought Turks along blood-soaked routes through Asia Minor (Anatolia) to the Holy Land. By the fourteenth century, with the Holy Land now beyond Christian reach, the Turks had become the targets of Crusades rather than obstacles in their path.

The Turks survived the first Crusades as well as the Mongol onslaught in the thirteenth century. In central Anatolia, the Mongols dealt a mortal blow to the Seljuk Turkish dynasty at Konya, but in western Anatolia smaller Turkish principalities survived and became independent of the Mongol Ilkhan dynasty. Osman, the founder of the most powerful of these, established himself around Söğüt in the far northwest. His followers (*Osmanli*) fought a ceaseless holy war (*ghaza*) against the Byzantine Empire. Later, under Osman's successor Orhan Gazi (1324-1359) the Osmanli, or Ottomans, crossed the Dardanelles into Europe to attack the Christian kingdoms of the lower Balkans.

Orhan established a bridgehead in Thrace, where he encouraged Turkish colonization and assembled forces for raids deeper into the Balkans. Because the Ottoman bridgehead in Thrace could be cut off from Anatolia, further expansion and consolidation were vital to its survival. Thus the Ottomans began the systematic conquest of all of Thrace, taking Adrianople, and transforming it into their first capital city in Europe, as Edirne, in 1361. The isolation and slow strangulation of Constantinople, an Ottoman vassal after 1363, had begun.

The next wave of Ottoman expansion into the Balkans came in the reign of Murat I (1360-1389), whose advance followed the geographical configurations of the Balkan peninsula. All roads led west; to the coasts of Albania by 1385, to Thessaly and Salonika by 1387; to Belgrade, by way of Sofia and Niş, a route that led to the destruction of the Kingdom of Serbia at the Battle of Kossova in 1389; and finally, a route north through the Balkan mountains. By 1388 Bulgaria and the Dobrudja had become Ottoman vassals.[1] Under Murat I Balkan Christians learned to fear Ottoman power in all its forms-from the fast-moving and destructive cavalry of holy warriors (*gazi*) to the highly disciplined armies of infantry and artillery often led by the Sultan himself. The western frontier was a moving frontier, establishing and coloring the Ottomans' relationship with the Europe beyond the frontier.

In the beginning of the fifteenth century, however, Murat's successor, Bayezit I (1389-1402) the Thunderbolt (*Yildirim*) attempted too much. Simultaneous expansion in Europe and Anatolia was as yet beyond Ottoman capacities. Gazi raiders spread death and destruction in Hungary, Bosnia, and Albania; and Bayezit won major victories in Serbia, Macedonia, Bulgaria, and Wallachia. He granted Ragusan and Genoese merchants permission to trade in his Empire, in return for tribute. He shattered one of the last Crusades, at Nikopolis, in 1396, and won control of the lower Danube from his rival the King of Hungary. In Anatolia, however, his campaigns alienated many Ottomans, who believd that fighting against Muslims violated the traditions of the *ghaza*. In 1402 he confronted the great Mongol warlord Timur, near Ankara. The Battle of Ankara echoed in European writing and drama for centuries, most prominently in Marlowe's *Tamburlaine the Great* (1587) and Nicholas Rowe's *Tamerlane* (1702). Another writer linked the historical event with the stage:

6

For with the losse of two hundred thousand Turkes against the valiant
Tamerlane he also lost his Freedome; and how he died, our stages have
instructed Mechanicall men.[2]

The defeat jeopardized the Balkan conquests, gave temporary
relief to Constantinople, and cast the dynasty adrift in an
interregnum that lasted until 1413.

Recovery would come with the redirection of Ottoman expansion to the European, western frontier. Mehmet I (1413-1421)
emerged as the sole ruler in 1413, partly because of the support
of the *gazi* leaders in the Balkans. They raided in Hungary,
Transylvania, and Bosnia throughout his reign. His successors,
Murat II (1421-1451) and Mehmet II (1444, 1451-1481), restored
unity to the Empire and consolidated central power within it.
Murat II smashed another Crusade, at Varna in 1444, and
Mehmet II ended the history of Constantinople, and began that
of Istanbul, in 1453. The conquest of Constantinople guaranteed
the geographical unity of the Empire, and was a prelude to the
annexation of Serbia, Bosnia, and Greece. Terrible *gazi* raids
into Carniola and Styria began in 1469. The mountain fastnesses
of Albania and Montenegro and the citadels of Belgrade and
Rhodes were beyond the reach of Mehmet the Conqueror, but
the Ottoman tide seemed irresistible everywhere else. Mehmet
eliminated the Genoese posts in the Aegean Sea, and annexed
the Morea. Ottoman raiders reached the outskirts of Venice.
Albania had been subdued by 1478, and the Ottomans landed in
southern Italy in August of 1479. Less noticed, but more
important for the future, was the extension of Ottoman control
over the Crimea. The Ottomans had taken the last Genoese
trading stations by 1478, and had won the right to appoint and
dismiss the Crimean Khans. The first Tatar and Turkish raids on
Poland followed in 1498. Bayezit II (1481-1512), pausing until the
death in Italy of his exiled brother Cem in 1495, went on to
establish the Ottoman fleet as a powerful offensive weapon. His
fleet attacked Venetian ships and possessions in the Aegean and
the Adriatic. By 1503 the Ottoman Empire had become the
colossus of the Balkans, and it also dominated the waters of the

7

Eastern Mediterranean.[3] Thus Bayezit's successor, Selim I (1512-1520), was able to attack the Ottomans' rivals in the Islamic East, defeating the Safavids in Persia and pulling down the Mamluks in Syria and Egypt. The conquest of Syria and Egypt doubled the size of the Ottoman Empire, and enabled still further growth by land and sea. Fighting to keep the old trade routes open, the Ottomans sent fleets into the Red Sea, past Aden, seeking the Portuguese in the Indian Ocean and at the Gulf of Hormuz. In the Western Mediterranean the Ottomans made contact with the Spanish Moriscos, and established naval bases along the North African coast. After Sultan Süleyman (1520-1566) entrusted the Ottoman fleets to the North African corsair Hayreddin in 1534, the Ottomans were within reach of mastering the whole Mediterranean. The naval struggle with Spain continued until 1580.

By land, Sultan Süleyman fought almost ceaselessly, in three campaigns in the East (1534-36, 1548-49, 1553-55) and ten in the West. He captured Belgrade in 1521, gaining the strategic initiative along the Danuble north to Buda. To protect his maritime communications with Egypt he took Rhodes in 1522. He added Mosul, Baghdad, Armenia, Yemen, Aden, Oran, Tripoli, and Algiers to the Empire. In Hungary he defeated and killed King Louis at the Battle of Mohacs in 1526, and briefly laid siege to Vienna in 1529. Most of Hungary became an Ottoman province and an Ottoman-Habsburg military frontier came into being. Behind the Ottoman frontier, the Balkan lands experienced what has been described as a *pax turcica*, while Ottoman political, military, economic and cultural institutions crystallized within the mold of military success.[4] The Ottoman Empire became a sophisticated and highly developed state, whose chief characteristics were: a society divided between a privileged military-slave elite and tax paying producers; the religious orthodoxy of the imperial establishment, particularly in relation to the perceived threat of Shia Islam; an army whose central units were either salaried or supported by "livings" (*dirlik*) i.e., grants of land (*timar*) held conditionally in return for military

8

service, the keeping of land registers and the promotion of good cultivation, trade and manufacturing; and an imperial culture embracing architecture, painting, poetry, music, and various traditional crafts. The distinctive appearance and manner of the ruling class was much described by European observers; the compendium of customary dress, language, bearing, and court ceremonial has been called "the Ottoman way." Less obvious to European observers was the Ottomans' indirect rule over the religious communities (*millet*) that made up the Empire. Some observers did cite examples of religious toleration in the Empire. But of all Ottoman institutions, the military was most obvious and important to European observers. They claimed, simplistically, that war was necessary to the well-being of the Ottoman state, as ballast for the ship of state. They saw the landed cavalry—"timariots"—as a remarkable force—vast, loyal, yet unsupported by imperial revenues. Most impressive, however, were the Janissaries, (*yeni çeri*) elite infantry, soldiers of Christian parentage brought into the Ottoman service in the periodic collection (*devşirme*) of youths made primarily in the Balkans. Those destined for the Janissary Corps became 'slaves of the Gate' (*kapikulu*), the standing army of the Sultan, well paid and trained in the use of firearms. Europeans knew them by their military reputation and by their services to them as guides and protectors. Their parentage made them objects of special fascination. The strength of the corps, indeed of the Empire, was linked in European eyes with the exclusion from the corps, and from the bureaucracy, of all but men of Christian origin.

Against such a background, the Christian naval victory at Lepanto in 1571 was shocking. It was the most celebrated triumph over the Turks before the Christian victory at Vienna in 1683. Ottoman losses were severe, and there were fears in Istanbul of a Christian naval offensive in the Dardanelles.[5] As a military success, however, Lepanto was incidental. Lepanto did not jeopardize the conquest of Cyprus, a prodigious effort and perhaps "the greatest feat of Ottoman arms."[6] By 1573 one author could see that the bloom was off the rose.

Certainlie it moveth me much to remember the losse of those three
notable Ilands [Rhodes, Chios, Cyprus] to the great discomfort of all
Christendome to those hellish Turkes, horseleeches of Christian blood.[7]

Under Selim II (1566-1574) and Murat III (1574-1595) the Ottoman navy recovered its strength; the Ottomans took Tunis in
1574 and Fez in 1576, menacing the Portuguese route to the
Indian Ocean, and threatening Spain's Atlantic route at Gibr-
altar and Seville.[8] In 1580, however, the Ottomans concluded an
agreement with Spain that ended the long struggle. Phillip turned
to deal with the Dutch and the English, while Murat III turned to
Hungary and the Caucasus.

The power of the Ottoman Empire to expand significantly by
land or sea at Christian expense was stalemated in the reign of
Mehmet III (1595-1603). The Ottomans made stupendous efforts
in their conquest of the Caucasus between 1579 and 1590, and in
a long series of campaigns in Hungary which began in 1593.
There, although the Sultan won a great victory at Mezokerestes
(Haç Ova) in 1596, he could not end the war. Fighting continued
until November 11, 1606, when both sides recognized stalemate
in the Treaty of Sitva Torok. The Ottomans renounced their
claims to Habsburg Hungary, and relinquished their annual
tribute from the Habsburgs. In the Caucasus, the Safavids had
recovered most of their territorial losses by 1613; the grim and
exhausting Ottoman efforts there had come to nought.[9]

What could explain the military stalemate? As early as 1585
Venetian ambassadors were seeing hopeful portents of Ottoman
decline.[10] Among modern writers, Fernand Braudel has suggested that the effects of climate and distances from Istanbul to
the various fronts sapped Ottoman strength: "the calendar was
commander in chief."[11] The relative decline of Ottoman power
has been attributed also to significant increases in population and
rising prices throughout the century. Behind the military frontiers the internal administration of the Empire began to falter,
and serious revolts against the Ottomans broke out in Anatolia.
Another evident change for the worse was in the character of the
dynasty. Lewis Thomas has described the period 1579 to 1656 as

"the women's Sultanate," in which power rested more often with the Palace establishment than with the Sultan.

Still, the Ottoman Empire remained a formidable and dangerous power at least until the end of the seventeenth century. There remained a durable framework for European military, diplomatic, and commercial relations with what Queen Elizabeth called "the most sovereign monarch of the East Empyre."

During the rise and expansion of the Ottoman Empire, Ottoman diplomacy played a role secondary to Ottoman arms. The traditional division of the world between the *Dār-ül-Islām*—the world of Islam—and the *Dār-ül-Harb*—the world of war—was characteristic of Ottoman frontier society, and continued into the more settled days of the seventeenth century. It implied continuous struggle on the frontiers of the Empire, and presupposed Ottoman superiority over the West. The Ottomans established no permanent embassy abroad before 1793, when their resident ambassador arrived in London. On the European side, therefore, it was imperative to maintain regular diplomatic representation in Istanbul, a venue satisfactory to Europeans and Ottomans alike. The Ottomans granted protection to all foreign visitors, and issued imperial documents of safe-passage, a *berat*. Travel within the Empire was restricted to those holding such a document.[12] Europeans might travel to Istanbul, reside there, and attempt to arrange an audience with the Sultan. Court interpreters were available from the staff of the *Reis Efendi*, responsible to the Grand Vizir, who oversaw all diplomatic business in the capital.[13] For European diplomats, the setting enhanced the degree of discretion necessary for diplomacy with the Turks. The medieval notion that Muslims ought not to be treated with and might lawfully be attacked, lingered on into the seventeenth century. Treaties among Christian states described their own conflicts as civil ones, to be ended in the face of the conflict with the Turks. The Turks were different in kind from Christians, a distinction not entirely justified under natural law, but surely justified under divine law. Within the *societas gentium*, Christians are as one against the enemies of Christendom.[14] Thus, the prologue of the Treaty of Vervins, 1598:

11

. . . the common enemy of the Christian name, taking our ills for his opportunity, and prevailing though our divisions, has made very great and dangerous progress and usurpations in the Christian provinces. . . .[15]

Nevertheless, in Istanbul the medieval coloring of diplomacy slowly faded. At the least, Europeans needed information about the Ottoman Empire. Beyond that there was the hope of establishing commercial relations with the Empire. Here Venice, "the vestibule to Islam,"[16] might be emulated. Of the European states Venice was reputedly the best informed in Ottoman affairs. Venice's situation was unique; the city's commercial ties with the Ottoman Empire survived its many wars with the Ottomans. Beyond both information and trade lay the possibility of establishing a formal alliance with the Turks, such as that concluded between Francis I of France and Süleyman in 1536. That alliance created the possibility of an Ottoman grant, to France, of commercial privileges in the Ottoman Empire.[17]

Commercial contact between the Ottoman Empire and the states of Europe rested on European demand for Eastern exports, the geographic position of Anatolia as land-bridge for east-west trade, the permanence of the Ottoman conquests in the Caucasus, the Arab lands, and the Balkans, and the economic policies of the Ottoman government. Eastern goods available to western exporters were well known. The Venetian ambassador Morosini listed them in 1585:

> From Constantinople go wool, leather, furs, and cambric; from Greece, cotton and spun thread; from Syria silk, ginger, spices, cotton, dyes, spun thread, pistachios, muslin, carpets; from Alexandria, spices, ginger, vegetables, dates, *bordi*, textiles, carpets, sugar and other things, and from the Mora, wheat and other grains.[18]

The Ottomans, aiming to achieve the highest possible level of imperial self-sufficiency, were willing to accomodate European merchants able to import goods in short supply in the Ottoman Empire, including materials of war.[19] They welcomed necessary imports, controlled their own exports, maintained internal communications, and generally fostered urban life. Towns of rela-

12

tively easy access to western merchants included Istanbul, Edirne, Bursa, Izmir, Aleppo, and, under different circumstances, Ragusa and Spalato. A network of overland trade routes and urban markets enabled the Ottoman Empire to enter the world market, as European merchants established themselves in the Ottoman Empire. They found the Ottomans willing to extend their protection and grant them charters of economic privileges (*imtiyazat*).[20] Europeans termed these grants "capitulations," a term derived from the Latin *capitulum* (a chapter). A capitulation was a unilateral grant of privileges, organized into chapters, awarded to merchants by the Ottoman government and subject to its renewal. The capitulations granted to France in 1569 specified the conditions of trade, the administration of justice within the merchants' community, and other extra-territorial privileges such as tax-exemption.[21]

In both diplomatic and commercial relations, Istanbul was the hub of the wheel. The city's role as a meeting place of East and West became proverbial. Rejuvenated by Mehmet the Conqueror after 1453, the city did seem to some Western visitors a malefic capital of a barbaric empire. But for merchants and diplomats it was also the goal of their long and difficult journeys, a city with recognizable features—classical monuments, Christian churches, European embassies—and unequalled vistas and opportunities. The Imperial Ambassador Busbecq described Istanbul as he saw it in the middle of the sixteenth century:

It stands in Europe but looks out over Asia and has Egypt and Africa on its right. . . . On the left lie the Black Sea and te Sea of Azof. . . . On one side the city is washed by the Sea of Marmara. . . . on the other . . . the Golden Horn. From the center there is a charming view over the sea and the Asiatic Olympus, white with eternal snow.[22]

Later descriptions took readers into the city and Topkapi Palace:

. . . there are in this city seven little hills upon . . . which are built seven principall Mosques or Churches, by severall Emperours, whereof the Fairest and most stately is that of Sultan Solyman. Upon the North side of the City, standeth the Grand Seigniour's Palace or Seraglio, com-

13

monly called by the name of the Port. . . . It is walled about, and within it are many gardens, orchards, meadows and woods. In this Seraglio the Grand Seigniour hath many chambers . . . richly appointed. . . . He hath six young men which attend his person. . . . In the morning they put into one of his pockets a thousand aspers and into the other pocket twenty duckats of gold . . . If he give not away that day is their Fee at night . . . Whensoever he goes to hunting or to any other exercise . . . his . . . Chief Treasurer still followes him with great store of money to give away.[23]

Istanbul was the heart of the world of Islam, the capital of an Empire of fascinating wealth and strange power. Emanating from the world of Islam, however, was a world of war whose steady westward advance was terrifying.

2

"That Mightie Feare"

The European reaction to the Turks grew from the initial perception of Islam and the "Saracens." It was a hostile perception, an image meant to inspire Christian religious fervor and spirituality. The continuing emphasis on theological differences, i.e., Muslim shortcomings, resulted in an enduring caricature of Islam and Muslims. John of Damascus, writing in the first half of the eighth century, depicted the Prophet Muhammad not as the founder of a religious faith, but as a false prophet. To John, Islam was heretical because it denied God's redemptive revelation through Christ.[1] From that point, Western writers went on to enumerate the shortcomings and weaknesses of Islam. More purely historical works, based on original sources, like William of Tyre's *Gesta orientalium principium* (1184) were rare and atypical. Pioneer work in Arabic studies begun in Spain in the twelfth century yielded Robert of Ketton's translation of the Koran in 1143, but the eventual result of these labors was "a closet literature for parochial Christian intellectuals."[2] European writing on Islam meant to expose the fraudulent claim of the False Prophet Muhammad, to lay bare the Muslim denial of the divinity of Christ, and to open believers' eyes to the Koran.[3] "Mahamet" was no prophet, yet his followers worshipped him as a god. If Saladin was in Dante's Limbo, Muhammad found eternal torment, with the sowers of discord, in the Inferno. The Koran was a compilation of hollow forms and ceremonies, a falling away from the true Word, a statement of heresy, or paganism. Often Christian literature dwelled on the alleged companions of Islam, vice and promiscuity. Writers condemned fraternization with Muslims as the dream of conversion died,

15

and stressed instead Christian vigilance in a conflict between truth and falsehood.[4]

As Turkish power grew, writers distinguished between them and other older Muslim peoples. In Christian eyes the Turks added a new militancy to Islam. As late as the eighteenth century Daniel Defoe wrote of "the Infidel House of Ottoman," and its destruction of Christianity in "above three-score and ten Kingdoms." Recalling the attack on Vienna in 1683, he described the "Green Ensigns of Mahomet and the Turkish Halfmoon on the Tops of their Spires, in the room of the Cross."[5] In the fourteenth and early fifteenth centuries, with the Turks now west of the Dardanelles, smashing the Christian kingdoms in the Balkans, isolating Constantinople before taking it in 1453, new life came to the older tradition of the Crusade. Schemes for an armed descent on the Holy Land were now impractical, but small forces could attack towns along the nearer coasts. Christian victories at Izmir (1344), Alexandria (1365) and Gallipoli (1366) were spectacular but incidental. Large forces fared much worse. The Ottoman Turks crushed two crusading armies deep in Ottoman territory, at Nikopolis (1396) and Varna (1444). After Varna, the idea of a great Crusade against the Turks declined except at Rome and at the Burgundian court of Phillip the Good (1419-1467). Men talked there of vengeance for Nikopolis and Varna, and later, for Constantinople. There were still hopes of establishing an ideal Christian Kingdom in the East, or of making contact with the Christian land of Prester John, described by Mandeville,[6] or of reinvigorating western kingdoms with the virtues of the knight on Crusade. Burgundian travellers in the Ottoman Empire prepared reports on proposed theatres of operations. The most detailed of these was that of Bertrandon de la Brocquière, the *Voyage d'outremer*. He cited many Turkish military virtues and suggested their imitation in Christendom. Turkish strength he attributed to chivalric Ottoman "knights;" their weakness lay in the large number of Christian renegades in their armies, men who would surely desert to a Crusading force.[7] No Burgundian Crusade materialized, and his theories went untested. There was no significant relief for Constantinople.

16

Throughout Christendom the reaction to the fall of the city was less shocked and fearful than was once supposed. Many writers blamed the Byzantines for the disaster. Some, calling the Turks the descendants of the Trojans, saw the fall of Constantinople as retribution for the fall of Troy. In any event, the peril was already well west of the Hellespont. In 1456 twelve thousand crusaders went to the defence of Belgrade against Mehmet II, but their success was again only incidental. The initiative lay with the Ottomans. In 1459 Pope Pius II (1458-1464) wrote:

> We found (and this will surely happen if we do not take care) that once the Hungarians were conquered, the Germans and Italians and indeed all Europe would be subdued, a calamity that must bring with it the destruction of our faith.[8]

In the second half of the fifteenth century, forming and directing a great Crusade became part of plans for Papal reform of the Church. Here the basic precept was that Turkish victories signified the spread of corruption within the Church and, later, the spread of heresy, Christian discord. A strong reforming Pope would work for peace within Christendom, inspire a Crusade, and rejuvenate the Faith.[9] An important corollary was to deny that the Turks themselves possessed any inherent strengths or virtues. Pius described them as "unwarlike, weak, effeminate, neither martial in spirit nor in counsel, their spoils taken without sweat or blood."[10] Again, theories went untested. Pius' death in 1464 at Ancona, where he had awaited the arrival of promised forces, has long been taken as an epitaph for the Crusading tradition. In 1529 Andrea Cambini described the end of the Pope's long wait:

> . . . in the meantime the fever dyd so growe and encrease upon him that the same day that the Duke of Venice landed in the haven of Ancona, accompanied with galleys and a great number of gentlemen he yielded up his soule to God. . . .[11]

The last great Papal champion of crusade before Pius V was Leo X. For him and his spokesman at the Fifth Lateran Council it was a "safe" topic, an antidote both to Christian disunity and to the severe external threat as well. The Papal Curia became a chief source of news of Turkish victories in the Balkans, in Syria, and in Egypt.[12]

The stunning speed of the Ottoman advance had outpaced and outlived the Crusading tradition. Belgrade was saved in 1456, and the tradition would live again in the victory at Lepanto in 1571, but Europe was now too diverse, and divided, for any significant force to be organized, let alone succeed. Political and religious developments within Europe from the fourteenth century on precluded any united military response to the Turks. Literary responses, while certainly hostile, reflected Europe's divisions, and diversity. The shifting currents of European civilization created a number of different perspectives on the Ottoman danger. One significant example lies with Renaissance humanists, seeking answers to fundamental questions: what is the origin of the Turks? what explains their successes? what is the proper response to them?

The idea that the Turks were descendants of the Trojans slowly yielded to the idea that they were descended from the ancient enemies of Greece and Rome, the Scythians. Both theories provided for a neat historical correspondence in vengeance—either for the sack of Troy or for the ravages of Alexander.[13] In neither case did questions of Turkish qualities and institutions arise.

Niccolo Machiavelli included the Ottoman Empire within the compass of *The Prince* (1513). As an example of an absolute monarchy dependent on slavery and a standing army, the Ottoman Empire was difficult to conquer but easy to hold.[14] Machiavelli applauded the fact that in the Ottoman Empire careers were open to men of talent.[15]

To Christian humanists such as Erasmus the Turkish conquests were a sign and consequence of the spiritual weaknesses of Christianity, for which neither Crusade nor pilgrimage was fit remedy. "Is it so very important," he asked, "that you make a physical trip to Jerusalem, when in your heart there is a veritable Sodom . . . ?"[16] He went on to suggest that instead of sending

18

"dull troops and companies" against the Turks, the *Res publica christiana* send "the brawling Scotists, the most obstinate Occamists, and invincible Albertists. . . ."[17]

Similarly, Thomas More saw the Turks as the image of spiritual malaise within Christendom. His *Dialogue of Comfort Against Tribulation*, (1534), set in Hungary on the eve of a Turkish invasion, did suggest a parallel between the impending fate of the author and his characters, but in a larger sense More meant to re-state and strengthen the argument of Erasmus: ". . . there is no borne Turk so cruell to Christian folke as is the false Christen that falleth from the fayth . . ."[18]

German images of the Turks in the divided and dangerous days of the early sixteenth century reflected religious divisions and, above all, fear. The Turk was the *Bluthund*, his hosts a *Schwärmerei*. "To Catholics and Lutherans alike, the Turk was like sin itself: he was a constant danger, and they worried about him."[19] Worry and fear—the *Türckenfurcht*—took many forms: *Türckenpüchlein*, (pamphlets) *Türckenlieder*, (songs) *Türckenglocken*, (bells) *Türckensteuer*, and the *Türckenpfennig* (taxes). The *Türckenlieder* were both "secular" and "spiritual." The former recorded battles and sieges, including the siege of Szeged in 1566, during which Sultan Süleyman died.

Entlich ist er gefollen hat sein Geist geben auf mit sein
Kriegs lauten allen der Feind schickt bald hinauff.

"Spiritual" songs portrayed the Turks as the essence of immorality and tyranny, and as the Scourge of God. Some invoked the story of David and Goliath, and others called for Christian unity in the face of peril. In the divided world of German Christianity the Turks soon became stock figures in theological debate and polemic. Luther at first interpreted Turkish victories over Christians as well deserved divine punishment, which ought to be owned up to and accepted, rather than resisted. The failure of the Crusades signified the error of Catholic doctrine. The Turk and the Pope were the arch-enemies of Christendom.[20] They were the flesh and spirit of the anti-Christ.[22] The shocking defeat of King Louis of Hungary at Mohacs in 1526 did justify to Luther a *Türckenkrieg*, a defensive struggle under the leadership of the Emperor: but ultimate relief awaited spiritual rebirth throughout the Church.[23] The polemical battles of lesser authors fighting to fix responsibility for Turkish victories on one faith or the other have been aptly described as "dead and dreary,"[24] and I will not go into them.

But the German reaction was not entirely one of fear, hatred, and polemic. The peril was not beyond political manipulation in the Diet.[25] Some writers, meanwhile, recognized the importance of studying Turkish institutions. In 1537 Philip Melanchthon wrote

> and since in this era a war has broken out in which we must fight the Turks, not only in defence of liberty, laws, and other refinements of civilization, but also for our religion, altars and homes, it is of the greatest importance for our princes to get a thorough understanding of Turkish affairs.[26]

Accordingly, by century's end, German translations of Ottoman chronicles began to appear in print.[27] There was also a body of travel literature, typified perhaps by the work of Salmon Schweigger. He left Tübingen in 1575, journeyed to Vienna and there joined an Imperial party leaving for Istanbul, where he remained a year. He admired Topkapi Palace, the great mosques, and the hostels, hospitals, schools, and baths supported by religious endowments.[28] He commented upon the exemplary behavior in the public baths, comparing it favorably with what might have been expected of Christians.[29] He was contemptuous of everything else. He described in lugubrious terms the fate of the Sultan's suppressed Christian subjects, and bemoaned the disrepair of the classical monuments of Istanbul.[30] For Schweigger, the Empire was simply the Scourge of God.[31]

French writings on the Ottomans flourished after about 1520. French authors wrote with the Valois-Ottoman alliance and the Capitulations of 1569 as background. They tried to analyze civil and military institutions, the administration of justice, and the intriguing practice of providing careers for men of talent. They cited examples of cruelty, but also examples of widespread sobriety, cleanliness, and tolerance. They noted a separation of moral virtue and religious doctrine.[32] Even so, many remained largely hostile. A good example is the travel account of Nicole de Nicolay, whose engraved illustrations have been often reproduced. His account appeared in English in 1585. He wrote that he had seen no human life in Turkey: ". . . it might better be called a life of brute beasts."[33] He described the Harem, though without seeing it.[34] In his eyes the Janissaries were "horrible, hideous, and fearful." Over all, he hoped that his descriptions would inspire a Crusade.[35]

There were many accounts by former prisoners of the Turks, many of which seem to have been widely read. The account of Johann Schiltberger, who was captured at Nikopolis in 1396, went through many editions in the fifteenth and sixteenth centuries. It did not appear in English, however, until the nineteenth century.[36] George of Hungary (Captivus Septemestrensus), captured at Mühlbach in 1438, wrote an account of his experiences first published in Latin and later issued in many corrupt German editions.[37] Another example that does not seem ever to have appeared in English was that of G.A. Menavino, who wrote of his experiences as a page in the Topkapi Saray. His description of the ideal Ottoman remains memorable:

> the warrior statesman and loyal Muslim who at the same time should be a man of letters, a gentleman of polished speech, profound courtesy, and honest morals.[38]

Probably the most significant and influential description of the Ottoman Empire in the sixteenth century was that of Ogier Ghislain in de Busbecq. He was hostile to the Turks but not close-minded. He went to Turkey for the first time in 1554 as Imperial envoy to the Sultan. He related his impressions of the Ottoman Empire in four letters in Latin which were not intended for publication, but did in fact appear, beginning in 1581, with an appendix, containing suggestions on how to fight the Turks. By

1700 the work had gone through twenty editions in seven languages, having appeared in English for the first time in 1694.[39] His letters contain a broad range of impressions and interests, from flora, fauna, and zoology to classical monuments and the Ottomans themselves. He wrote at great length about the struggle for succession among the sons of the Sultan; here, his narrative was an almost impenetrable fog of intrigues, speeches, soliloquies, victories, and defeats.[40] In other places, however, his writing was acute, informative, and attractive. He conveyed a sense of Turkish glamour, as in his description of the cavalry which met his party at the frontier near Gran:

> They formed a charming spectacle to my unaccustomed eyes, with their brightly painted shields and spears, their jeweled scimitars, their many colored plumes, their turbans of the purest white, their graments, mostly of purple or bluish green, their splendid horses and fine trappings. Their officers rode up and welcomed me with courtesy. . . .[41]

Further along the road, at Buda, Busbecq encountered Janissaries for the first time. He learned, he said, that they did garrison and police duties in the major cities of the Empire, protecting the weak and the poor of all religions. He found them unassuming and highly disciplined, and he compared them with monks, upright and armed.[42] He travelled along safe and well maintained roads. The Turks were "not unlike to great rivers, whose swelling waves having once broke through the obstacles that stopped them make a vast spoil wherever they come."[43]

Busbecq paused in Istanbul. The Sultan was not in his capital, but at Amasya, in the East. With no chance to conduct business, and afraid of the plague, Busbecq turned to describing marvels, such as a cameleopard and a two-headed turtle—"for seeing we were so disbarred of human society what better conversation could we have to drive grief from our minds than among wild beasts?"[44] He found the Turks to be primitive, and given to every extreme of manner and behavior. They were ill-natured, greedy, barbarous, and full of suspicion—attributes stemming from their devotion to a false faith. Topkapi made little impression on him, and the classical monuments he saw were few in number and poorly preserved.[45]

En route to Amasya he noted signs of discontent with Ottoman rule,[46] but all such thoughts disappeared when he reached the Sultan's encampment. His descriptions there portray the Ottomans at what was perhaps the summit of their imperial power:

> In Turkey every man has it within his power to make what he will of the position into which he is born . . . Those who hold the highest posts under the Sultan are very often the sons of shepherds and herdsmen . . . This is why the Turks succeed in all their attempts and are a dominating race and daily extend the bounds of their rule. Our method is very different. . . . everything depends upon birth. . . . You must regard these remarks as intended for your ears only.[47]

Busbecq's portrait of the Janissaries drawn up in ranks is a stunning image of Ottoman discipline in full flourish:

> The most remarkable body of men were several thousand Janissaries who stood in a long line apart from the rest, and so motionless that, as they were some distance from me, I was for a while doubtful whether they were living men or statues until . . . I saw them all bow their heads in answer to a salutation.[48]

Admirable as all this was, the danger to Christendom was immense: "'Tis only the Persian stands between us and Ruin."[49] He saw one hope; the Turks could be confused and disheartened by the superior firepower Christian forces sometimes brought to bear. Also he noted mutinous tendencies among the Janissaries.[50]

By the end of the century other writers, noting the increasing difficulties the Ottomans encountered in Hungary and the Caucasus, hoped that the Ottoman danger might now recede. In 1592 the Venetian ambassador wrote of the Ottoman Empire that "its decline may now be underway."[51] The Venetian physician Giovanni Tomasso Minadoi, resident in the Venetian consulates in Syria from 1579 to 1586, thought that the Ottoman victories in the Caucasus were Pyrrhic, and that they had fatally ruptured the stability of the Empire.[52]

Books in English on the Ottoman Empire began to appear just prior to the mid-century mark. These "Englished" translations and derivatives of works by Continental writers increased in number in the years following, and were joined in the last decade of the century by accounts of English observers and writers themselves.

The first important work on the Ottoman Empire in English was a translation of Antoine Geuffroy, *Estat de la Court du Grant Turc* of 1542. Geuffroy was a Hospitaller, and the work was published in Antwerp. Richard Grafton's translation, *The Order of the Great Turk's Court of hys menne of warre and of all hys conquestes with the summe of Mahumetes doctryne* appeared in London in 1544. The book described Istanbul and Topkapi Palace, and noted the chief doctrines of Islam. The author found some merit in Islamic monotheism, its recognition of the prophecy of Jesus, and its careful attention to the needs of the poor and the sick. As for the Turks, they are presumptuous and boastful, convinced of their superiority over all others. They are lazy and gluttonous.[53] They will receive all ambassadors, but send none.[54] They are secure in their isolation, destroying all fortifications and imposing severe taxes to grind their subjects down. They have few able men, no wisdom, strength, or virtue. They succeed as God punishes sinful Christians; they will be overthrown when God is pleased to reward a united Christendom with that task.[55]

Two years later Peter Ashton's translation of a Latin version of Paolo Govio's *Commentario de le cose di Turchi* (1531) appeared in England. Giovio, Bishop of Nocera, based his work on interviews with admirals, generals, diplomats, merchants, and former prisoners of the Turks.[56] Ashton's translation, *A Shorte Treatise upon the Turkes Chronicles, compyled by Paulus Jovius* . . . had three sections. The first dealt with the origins of the Turks, the second with the lives of the "Turkish Emperours," and the third with the organization and characteristics of the Ottoman armies. Giovio intended his work to be an instructive contrast between Christian heroism and Turkish cruelty. He believed that Turkish victories made his work more timely than ever before, but that ultimate Christian victory was inevitable.[57] The Turks' advantages—their own barbarism, their vast numbers of Christian slaves and renegades, and the discords of Christianity—were only temporary. Turkish "Emperours," save for Selim I, conqueror of the Arab lands, were counterparts of the ancient barbarian kings; Selim, however, brought to mind both Alexander and Caesar. He was severe, but a just defender of civil order, excellent in war and government, and risen in every conceivable way above the dark, Scythian Turks themselves.[58] In the third section, on Ottoman military strength, Giovio was less parochial and rhetorical. He noted the firearms of the Janissary corps and the masses of disciplined, fanatical, and Spartan-like soldiers. To resist them the Holy Roman Emperor should hire German mercenaries. The systems of provincial administration and land tenure complemented Ottoman military power.[59]

Turkish military virtues were noted again in Joannes Boemus' *Omnium gentium mores leges et ritus . . . Africam, Asiam, Europam* (1520), published in England in 1555 as *The Fardle of Facions*. He cited severe discipline, devotion to duty and order, and the cleanliness of their camps. For the rest, *The Fardle of Facions* was a bundle of polemic. It attacked Islam, and followed that attack with an invidious comparison between Islam and Catholicism. Even Islamic "men of religion" are more attentive to their flocks than Catholic priests are.[60]

Far more vivid and generally informative was Andrea Cambini's *Two Commentaries. The One of the Originall of the Turks. The Other of the Warre of the Turks Against George Scanderberg*, published initially in 1529 and in English in 1562.[61] The author hoped to explain how the Turks "attained to that mightie feare in the which they now fytte and commaunde, to the great dishonour of the Christian princes."[62] Cambini organized the first *Commentary*, on "the Originall of the Turks," into four books, each a chronological treatment of Ottoman conquests. He noted one source, an Italian "turciman" named John Cerini. He emphasized that barbaric cruelty and boundless ambition had been inherent in the "house of Ottomano" since Scythian times. He described the tremendous fury of Mehmet the Conqueror's final assault on the walls of Constantinople, saying "everye man foughte to gette up the wall, one clymynge on the others shoulder and up by their Pykes like Cattes. . . ."[63] Later he described the sack of Negroponte:

> . . . impalinge them upon long stickes, of others they pinched skin over their eares, and some others they cut a sunder in the middest. . . . All the streets of Negroponte were fylled with dede boddies and washed with Christian bloude. . . . They take all the inhabitants . . . and made them slaves, and when they had thus done, they began to sacke the towne both houses and churches. . . .[64]

Fortunately for Christendom, Selim I turned toward the East. Fearing the attraction "that the heresies of the 'Sophie,' " i.e., Şah Ismail (1502-1524), first Safavid Şah of Iran, might exert on the simple Turks, and hating the "Soldane of Egypt," i.e., the Mamluk regime in Syria and Egypt, for claiming the leadership of the "Mahometane" world, he attacked them both. This terrifying ruler quelled mutinies among the "Giannazzaries," recruited Christian gunners, and prepared his guns "lyke unto which the Christians use at this daye, wherefore he caused to breake all the great Bombardes . . . and caused to make a great number of Carriages."[65]

Former prisoners of the Turks left several accounts in English. The most important of these in the sixteenth century was that of Bartholomew Georgijevic. Captured at Mohacs in 1526, he remained a prisoner for thirteen years. His *De afflictione . . . captivorum* appeared first in 1544, and went through nineteen editions in German, French, Dutch, Polish, and English before the end of the century. Christendom's nemesis drew its strength from the levy of Christian, particularly Macedonian, children. Descendents of Alexander's soldiers make up the Sultan's Janissary Corps. Macedonian Janissaries "use long gunnes out of whych they shoute forth pelletes with great swiftness," he said. Georgejevic also described the *gazi* raiders, whose deeds he heard celebrated in Turkish verses.[66] Religion, he reported, bound the Sultan to lead all his forces against Christendom every third year.[67] Meantime, Ottoman courts of law, described as moralistic, severe, and quick, guaranteed stability to the state. The Ottoman economy, while not as "subtle" as that of Christendom, was vibrant and diverse, particularly in handicrafts. Merchants travelled throughout the Empire, and had a close and profitable relationship with the Venetians. The Turks themselves were barbaric, as their own folklore indicated. Their Empire was a great slave market in which they persecuted Christians without mercy or end, forcing their children to do the work of the Devil. Soon all traces of Christianity will have vanished.[68]

Gloom and hostility appeared again in the translation of Frauncis Billerbeg's *Epistola Constantinopoli redens scripta*, published first in 1582 and in English in 1585. The translation was newsworthy in its title alone: *Most rare and strange discourses of Amurathe the Turkish Emperour that now is. Of his personne, and how he is gouerned: with the warres between him and the Persians, and also of the Tartars and the Muscouites: of the peace concluded between King Philip and the great Turke: the Turkish triumph . . . with the confession of the Patriarch of Constantinople, exhibited to the Greate Turke.* According to this book, Murat III was a debased and frightful monster, surrounded and dominated by his harem and his "Sclavonian" slaves. Yet the Sultan's Christian peers were quarrelsome hypocrites. Philip's truce with the Ottomans, concluded in 1580, is their monument. That deed endangers honorable princes and leads desperate believers to "turn Turk."[69] The author described the celebrations held in Istanbul to mark the circumcision of the Şehzade Mehmed as pitiful festivities, fit for a people destined for Hell.[70]

The last significant work to appear in translation was *The Ottomano of Lazaro Soranzo*, which appeared in 1603. It was an unrelievedly hostile Crusading tract, describing the "head, members, and forces" of the Ottoman "body," its cogitations," and the dangers it posed to Christendom. The author likened Murat III to Caligula. His Empire lay in ruins, its economy weak, its navy a shambles, and its army now a mob of "country clownes."[71] Although the Janissaries are still well armed and "will fight resolutely for honour,"[72] the Ottomans expended much and gained little in their most recent campaigns in Hungary and Persia. They rely more and more on the "Tartars," descendants of those Israelites banished from Medea by the Persians.[73] The Empire stands on the brink of revolt. Christian and "natural Turks" hate their renegade masters, and soon the Janissaries will rise to reclaim their Christian birthright.[74] The decrepitude of the Ottoman navy endangers their communications with Egypt, yet Christian princes, particularly the English, do nothing. Those Christian merchants who trade with the Turks are worse, they are their prime source of information about Christian affairs.[75]

With Soranzo we conclude this summary of reactions to the "mightie Feare." Could English readers of the day have derived an image of the Ottoman Empire from the various works available in translation? There were at least two broad composites, each sharing a number of features. On the one hand, the Ottoman Empire was clouded in the dire gloom of a false religion. Until God brought about the rejuvenation of Christendom, the Turks would remain the whip in His hand. European authors had come to agree on the Scythian origins of the Turks, and stressed the misery of their Christian subjects. Most emphasized the importance of the Sultan's Christian-born slaves. They made up a standing army, in which merit counted above all. Most writers commented on the order and the discipline of Ottoman armies, and on the arbitrary nature of Ottoman justice. On the other hand, however, by century's end, the literature often portrayed the Ottoman Empire in a state of grotesque weakness and decadence. Christian rulers were exhorted to act. By that time, however, the English had become well established in the Ottoman Empire, and their interests lay in Ottoman strength rather than weakness.

3

The English Discovery of
The Ottoman Empire

Until the late sixteenth century, English interest in "the Great Turke, hys menne of warre" had grown slowly, at great distance. There was nothing in the English perception of Islam to prepare the ground for an accumulation of knowledge about the Turks; knowledge of them was almost nil in medieval England. Authors condemned Islam and used the terms "Turk" and "Saracen" almost interchangeably.[1] The use of terms relating to Turkey reveals an almost consistently derogatory association. The word "Turkey" seems to have appeared in English for the first time in Chaucer, in 1369. "The Turk" was generally used in reference to the Sultan, or as a symbol of Turkish power. The expression "to turn Turk" appears first at the close of the sixteenth century.[2] From the middle of the sixteenth century, "Turk" or "Turkish" was applied to anyone having the so-called qualities of the Turks, i.e., cruelty, unmanageability, and general barbarity; or "Turk" might be used as a name for targets on shooting ranges. It was often used as a name of origin or typology, as in names for horses, swords, and sabres. "Turkery" referred to Islam. As a verb form, there was the now obsolete German word *türcken*, to twist or writhe about, or to wrap about. It meant to change or alter, usually for the worse. In English: "Many [of these heretics] had the propre fayth to wry and torcass the Scryptures." Between London and Istanbul there stretched a sea of parochialism and a world of war. The title of a short work from 1515 shows the breadth of the former: *Here begynneth a lytell treatyse of the turkes law called Alco-*

ran. And *also it speaketh of Machamet the Nycromancer*. Perhaps the first English description from the world of war was an account of the siege of Rhodes, published in 1482. Such savage fighting was deplorable even at a distance: "To such beastly cruelties the noble feates of arms be come unto twixt the Christian men and the Turkes."[3]

There were English traders in the Ottoman Empire in the early sixteenth century. They offered woolens and kerseys for silk, pepper, and other spices, but were without any imperial dispensation or protection. In 1553 one merchant, Anthony Jenkinson, secured a safe-conduct or trading license, but he was more interested in Russian routes to Persian silk than in the trade at Aleppo or Istanbul.[4] Ultimately, however, the Ottoman Empire could not be ignored or by-passed. In the later 1550's and 1560's English merchants began to vault the world of war, coming to posts on the Caspian Sea and later to the capital itself.[5] In 1578 William Harborne,"a government agent under cover of trade" came, to Istanbul from London to secure trading privileges for English merchants, and to offer the export to the Ottoman Empire of war materiel. The Grand Vizir Sokollu Mehmet Paşa was receptive.[6] Soon further questions emerged: the naming of an English ambassador to the Ottoman Empire, and even the possibility of an alliance between the Queen and the Sultan against Spain. In a letter to the Queen written in March, 1579, Murat III promised security to merchants. The Queen replied to the "most sovereign monarch of the East Empyre," seeking confirmation of the latter point. In May, 1580, the Ottoman government granted English merchants Capitulations, securing their trade and legal privileges, giving England a status in the Empire equal to that of France and Venice. The document called for the release of all English prisoners in the Ottoman Empire, and entitled English consuls to the service of imperial interpreters.[7] In June, 1580 the Sultan confirmed the Capitulations.[8] The establishment of The Levant Company, with a monopoly for seven years, followed on September 11, 1581. Letters Patent from the Queen entitled the Company to the

. . . trade and merchandise and traffiques into lands . . . of the Great Turk . . . whereby there is good and apparent hope and likleyhood both that many good offices may be done for the peace of Christendom, and reliefs of many Christians that be or may happen to be in thraldome of necessitie under the sayde Grand Signior . . . and also good and profitable vent and utterance may be had of the commodities of our Realme. . . .[9]

Throughout 1582 the Company petitioned the Crown to name an ambassador, citing the trade it anticipated in spices, galls, cotton wool and yarn, chambletts, rice, soap, oils, hides, dates, drugs, linen, carpets and silk, damask, indigo, goat skins, and wax.[10] William Harborne accepted appointment on November 20, 1582 as the Queen's "Orator, Messenger, Deputy, and Agent."[11] The Company would bear his salary and expenses. He was to confirm the friendship between the two rulers, maintain the English privileges, create consulates where advantageous, and enact laws and statutes for the English in Turkey.[12] Murat III received him in May, 1583 and shortly thereafter reconfirmed the English privileges, with some favorable modifications.[13]

The new Embassy had been created at a time perhaps opportune for unorthodox diplomatic maneuvering. In 1580 England faced imminent war with Spain; Spain's struggle for the Low Countries threatened to spill across the Channel, and it was indeed the task of the Spanish Armada in 1588 to carry that struggle to English shores. The Queen, Harborne, and his successor Edward Barton seem to have worked hard to interest the Ottomans in allying with them against idolatrous Spain. One later author, relying on their correspondence, equates the importance of an alliance, in English eyes, with that of trade. The Queen's good name in Christendom was at stake, and diplomatic overtures were not to be advertised in Hakluyt's *Principall Navigations . . . of the English Nation*, where other, more purely commercial, documents from The Levant Company were to be seen.[14] But anti-Spanish diplomacy at Istanbul was enticing. In 1585 Francis Walsingham, Principal Secretary of State, urged Harborne to investigate the possibility of turning the Ottomans against Spain:

... the limbs of the devil being thus set against another, by means thereof the true Church and doctrine of the gospel may, during their contention, have leisure to grow to such strength as shall be requisite for the suppression of them both.[15]

English hopes were misguided, if not to say naive. There was entirely too much at stake for the Ottomans elsewhere, most notably in the Caucasus, for them to attack Spain in the Mediterranean. Major fighting against the Safavids in the Caucasus broke out in 1579, and continued into the next decade. The Ottomans won one of the great victories in their history in 1583 (The Battle of the Torches) and went on to establish their control as far as the Caspian Sea, including most of Armenia as well.[16]

English opportunities for the time being were limited to commerce and courtesies between the sovereigns. The trade in war materiel continued. From England the Ottomans obtained great amounts of tin, lead, bronze from bells broken up in the Reformation, copper, brimstone, saltpeter, and gunpowder, as well as great numbers of arquebuses, muskets, and sword blades. There were English arms merchants in Istanbul.[17] Also, there was correspondence between Queen Elizabeth and Safiye Sultana, mother of Murat III's successor Mehmet III (1595-1605). In 1595 the Queen sent gifts to mark Mehmet's accession; these included a carriage for Safiye and an organ for the Sultan built by Thomas Dallam.[18]

Thus the distance between England and the Ottoman Empire closed somewhat. The English Embassy at Istanbul became a vantage point on the East, and the impressions of those visitors present at the creation of direct contacts helped to shape and color English images of the Ottoman Empire. The English recognized the military colossus they saw about them, and thought they saw within it a commercial emporium. Their images were ones of strength, opportunity, and strangeness—anticipated, approached, entered. The diary of the organ-maker Thomas Dallam, who accompanied the Queen's gift to Murat III was not published until the late nineteenth century, but it conveys the sense of strangeness approached and entered in the

32

late sixteenth century. Dallam first played the organ in a room within the Sultan's hearing; then

> it was the Grand Sinyor's pleasure that I should let him see me play upon the organ. When I came within the door, that which I did see was very wonderful unto me. I came in directly upon the Grand Sinyor's right hand, some sixteen of my paces from him, but he would not turn his head to look upon me. He sat in great state, yet the sight of him was nothing in comparison of the traine that stood behind him, the sight whereof did almost make to think that I was in a different world.

Some weeks later, when the Sultan was in Edirne, a page -a Cornishman turned Turk- took Dallam through Topkapi Saray; he describes the events as follows:

> . . . then crossing through a little square court paved with marble, he pointed me to a grate in the wall, but made me a sign that he might not go thither himself . . . Through the grate I did see 30 of the Grand Sinyor's Concubines that were playing with a ball on another Court. At the first sight . . . I though thwy had been young men, but when I saw the hair of their heads hang down on their backs, plaited together with a tassel of small pearls hanging in the lower end of it, and by other plain tokens, I knew them to be women, and very pretty ones . . . I stood so long looking upon them that he which had showed me all this kindness began to be very angry with me. He made a wry mouth, and stamped with his foot to make me give over looking, the which I was very loath to do, for that sight did please me wondrous well.[19]

Beyond the Palace, throughout the Empire, the trappings and substance of military power were clearly to be seen. They were awesome, and for the moment, unknowable. Ottoman armies moved in disciplined response to the dictates of an unknown strategy in strange lands. Anthony Jenkinson described

> . . . the manner of the entry of Solyman the Great into Aleppo . . . Light horsemen very brave, clothed all in scarlett . . . Janizaries . . . slaves . . . all afoote, every one bearing his harquebuste . . . the Great Turke himselfe with great pompe, a magnificence. . . . in his countenance and gesture a wonderful Majestie, having only on each side of his person one page clothed with clothe of golde; he himselfe was mounted on a goodly white horse, adorned with a robe of clothe of gold.

> All this aforesaid Armie, most pompous to behold, which was in number foure score and eight thousand, camped about the city of Aleppo. . . . The rest of his armie passed over the mountains of Armenia . . . [in] the number of 300,000 men.[20]

There were other, more mercantile attempts, to bring a power otherwise beyond comprehension "down to earth." Thus William Harborne's computation of the Sultan's expenditures: his "brief extract specifying the certaine daily payments . . . of the Grand Signior" came to "one million nine hundred three score eight thousand seven hundred thirty five pounds nineteen shillings eight pence."[21] From the Ambassador's perspective, the Ottoman Empire was a distillation of corruption. He warned James Towerson, whom he appointed to a consulate in Ankara, to find

> the most honest broker that you can gett, but trust him not too fare . . . nether yet seeme altogether to mistrust him least he greave it and maliciously deale with you but use him or them. . . . You are amongst your enemiyes for that nether Jew greek or venetian but will be prided with envie . . . for they all be a subtill, malytious and unfaithfull people whom you must overcome throughe god's grace. . . .[22]

The most important compendium of early English images of the Ottoman Empire came from John Sanderson, a merchant, traveller, and sometime diplomat. His autobiography, journals, and letters did not come to light until the nineteenth century. He was in Istanbul for six months in 1585 as Harborne's steward. Before he returned to England in 1588 he visited Egypt. In 1591 he was back in Istanbul, and in 1596 served as deputy to the second ambassador in Istanbul, Edward Barton, while Barton was in Hungary with the Sultan's army. From 1599 to 1601 he served as treasurer of The Levant Company.[23]

His descriptions were nothing if not vivid. The animals in the royal menagerie fascinated him:

> . . . I had the view of many animals, as oliphants, tame lions, tame spotted catts as big as little mastiffs, great and smaule deere. . . . The admirablest and fairest beast that I ever sawe was a jarraff. . . . This

fairest anymale was sent out of Ethiopia to this Great Turk's father as a
present. To Turks the keeper . . . would make him kneele, but not before
any Christian for any mony.[24]

The accession of Mehmet III in 1595 was macabre:

. . . Sultan Murad deceased the 7th of this month [January, 1595], and
was buryed the same day his sonne Sultan Mahemmet arrived . . . the
17th. That day his 19 sonns were strangoled in their brothers presence.
. . . We sawe them passe by to buryall; which was to be pitied, being
innosents, thoughe Turks. . . .[25]

The triumphant return of the new ruler from the victories in Hungary evoked this description:

. . . the Turke returned in great triumph; entered at Adrianople Gate;
three or four miles without which gate, and so long within the citie to the
gate of the Seraglio . . . four or five miles furder, all one both sides the
ways as he should passe throughe the people his subjects Turks, Jews,
Christians, held in length whole pieces of cloth of gould, velvett, sattin,
and damask. . . . and for three days together feasted, keeping open
shoppes and houses day and night. . . .[26]

He compiled a separate, descriptive guide to Istanbul, portraying it as a city whose life spanned two civilizations:

Constantinople in time past had eleven gates . . . but the continual fiers
and the many earthquakes . . . overthrew the famous auntient waule.
. . . Sultan Baizett gathered together more than 60,000 men to rebuild it,
making new gates. . . . following ar the names at this present . . .[27]

Among the great mosques of the city he singled out the mosque and hospices of Mehmet II:

Marvellous is the greatness and magnificence of it, being made in the
similitude of the Sofia, [the Cathedral of St. Sophia] and hath about it 100
houses covered with lead, of a round cube fation ordeyned to recieve
straungers and travailers of what nation or religion soever be, where they
may rest . . . three days . . . not paying anything. . . . Besides ther ar
lodgings where they give seropp and medizens of free cost . . . and
another for the government of the madd people.[28]

The city is also full of very faire banies [baths], as well publique as private, which, in imitation of the auntient Greeks and Romaines, ar built and contrived with great industery, sumptuousness and expence almost incredable . . . beutified with pillors, banks, and pavements of divers and rare colored marble. Faire they ar, and very great, with plentie of water.[29]

Finally, Sanderson noted the punishment meted out to rebels and traitors:

We have seen the traitor Ussine Bassa upon the gaunch . . . having one of his armes and a legge broke, and carried bound to a crosse of woode with two candles burning in the fleche of his shoulders, having also a muskle or two of fleche taken out of his backe, with a chope behind the nape of his necke. Dead he was before he was put on the gaunch.[30]

Another observer from the early days of the English presence in Turkey was Fynes Moryson. Though his *Itinerary* was published in 1617, it contained a great deal of information on the Turks which the author had collected on a short visit in 1596. Moryson was a serious tourist. He had taken a B.A. and M. A. at Peterhouse College, Cambridge and had been admitted to Oxford, but had decided to travel in Europe and to write a survey of conditions there. His travels included a short stay in the Ottoman Empire. He was the first English author to attempt to write a comprehensive survey of the Ottoman Empire. He began his account with a sprint through Islamic and Ottoman history, covering the centuries between the Prophet and the Sultans in ten pages. Relieved of that, he passed on to the first of his major themes, the nature of the Ottoman state, where he announced: "The form of the Ottoman Empire is merely absolute and in the highest degree Tyrannical, using all his subjects as born slaves."[31] In fact, the Ottoman Empire was no "tyranny" in Moryson's sense. Within the ruling class the Sultan's powers were theoretically nearly absolute, and he played a vital role as the "common focus of loyalty" within the Ottoman system. In practice, however, his absolutism was often only symbolic, limited by the "corporative substructure of Ottoman society,"[32]

36

and by law. Ottomans looked on the reign of Sultan Süleyman (1520-1566) as the period in their history most characterized by the strict rule of law, and referred to the Sultan as *Kanuni*, the lawgiver. In the Ottomans' "Circle of Justice," a traditional guide and statement of good government dating back to the eleventh century, the welfare of the state depended upon the welfare of the subject, producing classes. The Sultan's officers were not to exceed the limits of their authority.[33] Moryson believed that there was no true nobility even partially immune to the ruler's tyranny. The Ottoman "nobility" was made up of new men, of low birth and little security: "Like players on a stage they carry themselves for the short and slippery tearme of life."[34]

For all others, the Ottoman Empire was a great slave market. Turks regularly burnt Christian towns to the ground, to take a few chosen survivors into slavery. All Ottoman institutions were, to Moryson, extensions of tyranny. The most significant sources of imperial revenue, he claimed, were tyrannical confiscations, extortions, and arbitrary increases in customs dues.[35] In fact, the Ottoman tax system was based on the distinction between the Ottoman ruling class, who collected taxes, and the Sultan's subjects, who paid. The Sultan could alienate sources of revenue to Ottomans, and delegated power for that purpose. Taxes themselves including the hend tax (*cizye*) on Christians, were justified in Islamic law (*Şeriat*) or based on the Sultan's sovereignty. Most taxes in the latter category were fixed on the basis of land and populations, customary rates, and the conditions of land tenure.[36]

Among the chief officers of the realm only the soldiers are significant, Moryson wrote. He had heard of bureaus filled with clerks, but furnished only a long list of imaginatively spelled titles of offices, lists of functions, and salaries.

Amidst unmistakeable signs of Ottoman strength Moryson found portents of future weakness. The Janissary Corps presented a paradox: unlike European soldiers, they were generally respected in peace time. In their distinctive uniforms they were as fierce as mastiffs, absolutely reliable guides and interpreters for Christians and Turks alike. Yet the days when entry to the Corps was limited to those of Christian parentage alone were gone. "Soft Asians" were now in the ranks. The numerical strength of the Corps was never greater, and its military effectiveness never lower.[37] Moryson also discussed the landed cavalry, the "timariotti". Greed now corrupted the Ottoman system of vassalage, once more effective than any ever practiced in Europe.[38] The result here too was that Ottoman forces were numerically stronger than Christian forces, but were technologically inferior to them. In this sense guns and gunpowder have been a great asset to mankind. The Sultan relied on his "tartars;"[39] Christendom meantime, must hope that the Janissary Corps will become a "Praetorian Guard," more dangerous to the Emperor than to his enemies. Every tyranny in history has eventually fallen of its own weight, and the Ottoman Empire would be no exception.[40]

In the time remaining to it, however, the Ottoman Empire offered Western merchants a rare opportunity. Ottoman war and tyranny, Moryson wrote, had extinguished the spirit of enterprize among the Sultan's subjects; the Sultans wasted the great commercial potential of their lands. Any prosperous Turkish merchant might see his wealth confiscated at any time by the government. Greeks, Jews, "confederate Christians," and enterprizing Englishmen should sieze the economic opportunities created for them by Ottoman despotism. Their only risk was in being entrapped or captured and forced to turn Turk.[41]

The early seventeenth century was rife with tales of men captured at sea by the Turks, and forced into slavery as oarsmen in the galleys. According to one estimate, pirates took 466 English ships between 1609 and 1616. Not even the English coasts were safe.[42] There was a vast literature, of fleeting images, of adventure, cruelty, escape or deliverance. *A letter contayning the admirable escape and glorious Victorie of Nicholas Roberts Master, Tristram Stevens and Robert Sucksbich Boatson of a Ship of Dover, taken by Algier Pyrates: which three men being carryed as Slaves by eleven Turkes in the same ship partly killed and partly sold them all, all returned free and safe home into England* was a typical title; Edward Webbe's *The Rare and Most Wonderfull Things which Ed. Webbe . . . hath Seen and Passed . . .* (1590) described his imprisonment in the Ottoman galleys and his eventual release through the intercession of William Harborne. There were English free-booters and adventurers throughout the Mediterranean. The tale of the English ship *Dauphin*, attacked by three corsairs in 1616, is instructive—the pirate captains were Englishmen. There were stories of fights off the English coasts, including John Taylor's *A valorous and perillous seafight with three Turkish ships on the coast of Cornwall* (1640).[43]

Turks were found also in Elizabethan history plays, dramatic and didactic presentations of historical events and personalities.[44] The best known example, Christopher Marlowe's *Tamburlaine the Great*, recalled the titanic struggle for mastery of the East between Timur the Lame and Bayezit the Thunderbolt. Of the two, Timur (Tamburlaine the Great) is pre-eminent. His ambition drives him to destruction, while the Sultan is treated more sympathetically. Marlowe's *The Jew of Malta* recalled the career of Joseph Nasi, the Duke of Naxos, a confidant of Selim II.[45] Robert Green's *The First Part of "The Tragicall Reigne of Selimus* (1594) depicted the murderous steps by which Selim I, the Grim, came to power; murdering his brother, poisoning his father, and strangling his remaining relatives.[46] Thomas Kyd's *The Tragedy of Soliman and Perseda* (1599) is a tragic romance with the Sultan as villain.[47] In Shakespeare's *Henry V* the King assures Katherine, daughter of the defeated Charles VI, that their son would be a young lion who "shall go to Constantinople and take the Turk by the beard."[48] "The malignant and turban'd Turk" is well known; in *Othello* the "Ottomites" represent unrelenting, calculating danger:

We must not think that the Turk is so unskilfull
To leave that latest which concerns him first,
Neglecting an attempt of ease and gain
To wake and wage a danger profitless.[49]

The most enduring monument to Elizabethan interest in the Ottoman Empire was Richard Knolles' *The Generall Historie of the Turkes, From the First Beginning of that Nation to the rising of the Ottoman Empire, with all the notable expeditions of the Christian Princes against them, Together with the Lives and Conquests of the Ottoman Kings and Emperours*, 1603. The work came at the end of Elizabeth's reign, and was dedicated to the new King, James I. Knolles praised the "Heroicall Song" which the King had written as a boy to celebrate the Battle of Lepanto. Knolles never visited Turkey, and had little to say about those who had. But he had a great impact. The first edition contained nearly 1200 pages; the fifth, of 1638, which had been continued by others after his death in 1610, was nearly 1600 pages long.

Knolles was a schoolmaster at a grammar school in Sandwich. He made a reputation there as a man who did well by his boys, sending many of them on to universities. A friend, Sir Peter Manwood, encouraged him to write *The Generall Historie*, which Knolles hoped would show the "strange and fatal Mutations" which enabled the Turks to expand their Empire, by pulling together the "whole Tragicall historie" for the first time. He wrote for the advancement of the "Common State of Christendom." His work shared the common goals of Tudor and Stuart historiography, intended to teach "morals, manners, prudence, patriotism, statecraft, virtue, religion, wisdom and truth."[50] Samuel Johnson praised the work for deftly handling "a wonderful multiplicity of events" displaying "all the excellence that narration can admit." Later still, Byron wrote:

> Old Knolles was one of the first books that gave me pleasure when I was a child; and I believe it had much influence on my future wishes to visit the Levant, and gave perhaps the oriental colouring which is observed in my poetry.[51]

Today's reader senses its impact as one of weight, and length. It gives the impression of a very old and immense monument to soldiers, cities, and kingdoms fallen in forgotten wars, in remote places. The book is a narrative of campaigns and battles, closely described but integrated only by. the reigns of the Sultans. Princes, "bassaes," kings, and emperors meet in battles so titanic and remote that their actuality is hard to comprehend. War is an imperative of religion; corollary motives were the dictates of honor, the need for revenge, the necessity of rebuking "insolence," and the grasping, aggressive nature of the Ottoman Empire itself. The work is a panorama of war from which great lessons and moral truths emerge in the end. Five centuries of war are framed in great historical contrasts, which Knolles fitted in his opening section and in a concluding "briefe Discourse on the greatnesse of the Turkish Empire. As also wherein the greatest strength thereof consisteth." One such contrast was between the earliest Turks, a "wandring and unregarded People" and the present Ottomans, the "Terror of the World." Another was between the single-minded, conquering Ottoman state, and the divided and weak states of Christendom. With so little resistance along their frontier, the Ottomans came to recognize the "sinews of every well ordered commonwealth, Reward propounded to the good, and punishments threatened unto the Offender. . . ." They then perverted them to their own malevolent ends. They devised a devilish tax, to be paid in children, to turn the best of their Christian subjects into powerful slaves, loyal to their master. Thus, from the early state of Osman, "another Romulus" grew the present Ottoman Empire, greater than any other in history, "the Romane Empire only excepted."

Knolles' sources were of course wholly Western: Giovio, Latin translations of Ottoman chronicles, so called, by German authors, Minadoi, Lavardin (*The Historie of George Castriot*, London, 1596) and Boissard (*Vitae et icones sultanorum*, Frankfurt, 1596), Knolles wrote that he was disappointed in Ottoman sources, "from whom the greatest light for the continuation of the Historie was in reason to have been expected, [they] being . . . rather short, rude notes . . . , hard if not impossible to reconcile."

Knolles' narrative might be likened to a historical play, whose acts are the successive reigns of the sultans, and whose stage shifts from Hungary to Persia, from Cyprus to "Valachia." Through the entire work, the narrator spoke as a chorus to clarify the dire results of supernatural causation, Ottoman strength, and Christian discord. The "uncertaintie of worldly things" and the "Just and Sacred Judgement of the Almighty" deliver the innocent into Turkish hands, while religious war in Europe prolongs their misery and postpones their deliverance. The Turks are constant; they mean to conquer the world.

The first narrative section of the work discussed the Turks' origin, Scythian rather than Trojan, and "the ruine of the Turke's First Empire in Persia." Then, beginning with Osman, Knolles allotted a chapter to the life, deeds, and fatal flaws of each "King" or "Emperour." He began each with a bit of verse set beneath an engraving of the ruler. Following a description of battles won and lost, the section ended with a physical description of the ruler and an enumeration of the inevitable flaws in his character. There are chronological tables to show the parallel reigns of Christian rulers.[52] The fifth edition, of 1638, included the "briefe Discourse . . ." already noted.

The chapter on Osman draws distinctions among the Turks of the thirteenth century. Osman was not a "Selzuccan" (Seljuk) Turk, but instead an "Oguzian (Oğuz) one amongst many others of the Iconian (Konya) Sultan's subjects.[53] He was ruthless and opportunistic in the face of enemies blind to their own danger:

With endless wars the Asian states are spent and overworn . . .
The Christians draw their bloudy swords, wherewith themselves to wound . . .
[He] lays the Fatall plot whereon the wasteful Turke should raigne
And bathes his scepter in much bloud of people by him slain.

Knolles saw clearly that the first Ottomans were not a barbarian horde but that they built their Empire carefully. Areas long desolate under the "dead sleep" of the Byzantines sprang to life under their rule. Osman was never rash in his attempts. . . . [and] what he took in hand he commonly brought to good effect. . . . With great industry [he] laid the foundation of his Empire in Phrygia and Bithniya, now the greatest Terror of the World.[54]

Knolles had few words for Osman's successor Orhan, except to say that he was put on the throne by a "Parliament"—a body which failed to re-appear in his work. In the "Life of Amurath" (Murat I, 1360-1389) he described the origins of the Ottoman child levy, the *devşirme*. Knolles explained that every fifth Christian prisoner over the age of fifteen went to the "King." His men collected boys and distributed them among Anatolian farmers, who taught them the language, manners, and religion of their masters. The best of them became "Janizaries . . . , the greatest strength of the Turkish Empire," and eventually the foundation stone of tyranny:

The Grand Seignior's government is so absolute, as they all tearm themselves his slaves, and no man, how great so ever can assure himself of his estate, no not of his life . . .[55]

Murat's reign ended with his death after the great Ottoman victory at Kossovo in 1389. Knolles' description of the battle typifies his writing at its best:

. . . Many fell on both sides; the brightness of the armour and weapons was as it had bin the lightening: the multitude of the launces shadowed the light of the sun . . . the noise of the instruments of war, with the nighing of horses and the outcries of men was so terrible and great that the wild beasts in the mountains stood astonied . . . and the Turkish histories . . . vainly say, that the angels in heaven amazed with that hideous noise for that time forgot the heavenly hymns. . . .[56]

The reign of "Baizet, the First of that name, the Fourth and Most Unfortunate King of the Turks," was a "mirror of mishap."[57] Knolles attributed his defeat at the Battle of Ankara in 1402 to the flaws in his character. He was fortunate only in his successors, who saved the Ottomans from the ruin which befell the dynasty of Timur.

Knolles passed over Mehmet I and turned to Murat II (1421-1451). Murat perfected the system of enslaving Christian boys, "a great policie proceeding from a deep judgement" to bypass and degrade his "natural subjects" and to rely instead on his Christian subjects,

> the better part of them whom we cal Turks (but are indeed the children of Christians, seduced by their false instructors). . . . There is not one natural Turk among all those that bear authoritie. . . . Turks live in Anatolia, all of them either merchants, or of base and mechanicall trades, or poor laborers with the spade and pickax—and such like peoples unfit for the wars. . . .[58]

Most notable in the chapter on Mehmet II (1451-1481) was Knolles' account of the siege of Constantinople, "among the greatest calamities that ever happened to any Christian city in the world."[59] With its capture, the Ottoman "King" became an "Emperour." Then, at the summit of his power, Mehmet the Conqueror met "Venus," and was nearly defeated. In the presence of the beautiful captive Irene, "his Fierce nature was well tamed . . . [and] he was at war with himself." He gave up "the instruments of war" and virtually ceased to rule at all. With his armies straining to attack Belgrade, he dallied. Not until threatened with mutiny in the ranks did Mehmet act to reclaim his future. He planned carefully and acted swiftly. He

> made more of her than ever before,
> and the more to please her dined with her,
> commanding that after dinner she should be atyred
> with many more pretious jewels of inestimable value,
> whereunto the poor soul gladly obeyed, little thinking
> that it was her funeral apparel.

In the presence of his captains he struck off her head, saying: "Now by this judge whether your Emperour is able to bridle his affections or not.[60]

Preparations for the attack on Belgrade in 1456 began immediately. Knolles was glad to describe the successful defence of that city. It seemed as if the terrifying pressure might relent, as Knolles went on to describe the victories of George Kastriot (Scanderbeg) over the Turks and the inhuman cruelties of Vladus Dracula of "Valachia."[61]

The following reign of Sultan Baizet II (1481-1512) was a troubled one for the Ottomans. The rise in the East of "Hysmael" (Şah Ismail, 1487-1524), the founder of the Safavid dynasty in Iran, and his aggressive followers, the "cusselbas" (kizilbaş) was good news for Christendom. It was too much for Bayezit. The Sultan,

For worne with trembling age and civil discourd anew
Thrust from his Empire by his sonne
Died poysoned by a Jew.[62]

In "The Life of Selymus . . ." (Selim I, 1512-1520), Knolles concentrated on the eastern conquests of the terrible new ruler. His account of the defeat of Şah Ismail at the Battle of Çaldiran in 1514 exemplifies again Knolles' finest writing style. The Ottomans triumphed because of their "cruell, cowardly, and murthering artillery." It was artillery again which destroyed the "moderate and happy" government of the Mamluks in 1516. Yet Christendom was spared again, by the "loathsome canker" which caused Selim's death in 1520.[63]

Knolles' treatment of the reign of Süleyman (1520-1566) is not memorable. Over a hundred fifty pages deal almost wholly with battles won and lost in Hungary. Nowhere else in Knolles' work is focus and direction more needed. In the reign following, of Selim II (1566-1574) Knolles stressed the Ottoman defeat at Lepanto (October 7, 1571) and the Ottoman conquest of Cyprus in 1570-1571 as object lessons in Christian unity. When the news of Lepanto arrived in the West, "great was the joy conceived of the victory but to none more welcome than to the poore Christians just chained to the Turks galleys, of whom twelve thousand were thereby delivered." Francis Bacon compared Lepanto with Augustus Caesar's victory at Actium in 31 B.C., but Knolles saw Lepanto for the passing moment that it was:

"Defeat there was to the Turks like the loss of a beard, but to Venice, the loss of Cyprus was like the loss of an arm."[64] Still, the next Sultans (Murat III, 1574-1595, and Mehmet III, 1595-1603) were anxious for peace. Their advisors urged them to war, however, convincing them that war was necessary to sustain the strength of the Empire.[65] Knolles catalogues their conflicting recommendations about where best to fight; Hungary, and the Austrian Habsburgs became the most important objectives. It seemed evident, however, that the Ottomans had extended themselves to the utmost. "These doubtful wars of Hungary, with the general revolt of Transylvania, much troubled Mahomet the great Sultan, but nothing like unto the wars he had in Asia . . ."[66] Both Sultans were overwhelmed by their responsibilities, diverted by their courts, and used up by their own system of slavery. Mehmet III died

> a loathesome lump of dead Flesh . . . a man of no great spirit, and yet exceeding proud, which was the cause that he was both less beloved and feared . . . the men of warre . . . grieved to see even the greatest affairs of his state not only imparted to women but by them managed . . .[67]

The fifth edition of 1638 included continuations by later authors, as well as Knolles' discourse on Ottoman strength. He stressed the Ottomans' martial virtues, but also their great numerical strength. The number of the landed cavalry was given here as 719,000 (elsewhere in the work as 150,000), a figure the author claimed entailed no expense whatever to the Sultan.[68]

Overall, Knolles suited late Elizabethan tastes well, and he remained popular well into the seventeenth century. New editions, with continuations, appeared in 1610, 1621, 1631, 1638, 1687-1700 (in three volumes), and an abridgement, in 1701. Its appeal lay in the battle pieces, the staunch religiosity and moralizing conclusions, and with the writing style. It was "pure, nervous, elevated, and clear" according to Samuel Johnson, who rated Knolles above the Continental historians of the preceding century. Most important, the work gave the stamp of definitiveness. A difficult, yet important subject, had been nobly, and finally, explicated. Readers might feel in full command of the Ottoman world, in its long past and its present condition. There remained only the future, and continuations of the narrative would follow smoothly.

After finishing the first edition of 1603, Knolles turned to a new endeavor, the translation of a major work in European intellectual history. This was Jean Bodin's powerful argument for political sovereignty and stability, the *République*, 1576. Knolles' title was *The Six Books of a Common Weale*, published in 1606. In an earlier work Bodin described Islam as a faith with spiritual content as sell as ceremonial form.[69] Now, in the *République*, he pointed to the Ottoman Empire as an example of civil harmony within a truly sovereign state. He considered the Ottomans from two standpoints-government and climate. In the first, the determining factors were slavery and nobility, peculiarly combined.

> For as concerning the Turks' Praetorian Soldiers, and those youths which are taken from the Christians as tribute . . . I never accounted them slaves . . . They alone enjoy the great honours, offices, and priesthoods . . . All their posteritie afterwards being accounted base except by their vertue and noble acts they maintain the honour of their grandfathers, for the Turks alone of all other people measure true nobilitie by vertue, and not by descent or the antiquitie of their stocks: so that the farther a man is from vertue, so meuch the farther hee is . . . from nobility.[70]

Bodin described the Ottoman government in different ways. In Book II he linked it and the Muscovite monarchy, as "lordly monarchies" in which the rulers are lord over the goods and persons of their subjects, to whom they grant use of the land.[71] The Ottoman monarchy was also an hereditary one, and one of the "well ordered common weales."[72] Islam moderated Ottoman policies.

> The great Emperour of the Turks doth with as great devotion as any prince in the world honour and observe the religion by him received . . . yet deterreth hee not the strাunge religions of others; but to the contrary permitteth every man to live according to his own conscience.[73]

When Bodin turned to climate, and geography, he sacrificed most of his clarity. He included the Turks, with the Huns, Goths, and "Tartars," among those who sought in vain to dominate the northern and western portions of the globe. The Turkish occupation of former Assyrian and Roman provinces, in the "middle lands," is only temporary.[74]

Knolles agreed. *The Generall Historie's* later sections are full of images of great power, but contrasted with ultimate downfall and ruin. In the end, the image left by Knolles as author and translator is of "the shell of the Empire declining from its pristine greatnesse."[75] The outcome of a long history of war and statecraft is clear. Over Mehmet III (died 1603) Knolles intoned:

> Yet sith thou knowest not aright
>   For grace by Christ to call,
> All that thou boast's Mahomet
>   Is nothing worth at all.[76]

Knolles died at the beginning of the reign of Ahmet I (1603-1617), but his work described portents of ruin from early in the reign. In Istanbul the night skies were inauspicious: ". . . such strange meteors and Apparations being often times the Presages of the Ruine of them to whom they appear."[77]

4

The Ghost of Osman

After the English "discovery" of the Ottoman Empire in the late sixteenth century, the number of books on the Ottomans increased rapidly. The major thread was Knolles, and the continuations. Running through the first decades of the century, it was joined by important works by other authors, up to the mid-century mark.

Traditional hostility to the Ottomans did not wane. The new King, James I, was England's most prominent enemy of the Turks. His boyhood poem, "The Lepanto", had celebrated the victory over the Turks as God's victory over Satan.[1] The Turkish policies of Elizabeth meant little to James. He said that "for merchants' causes he would not do things unbefitting a Christian prince."[2] Ottoman visitors to his court got short shrift.[3] With Europe at war after 1618 he worried about the strength of the "Germaine nation", the "Bulwarke of Christendom." Quick estimates of Ottoman strength, such as John Finet's *The Beginning, Continuation, and Decay of Estates* (1606) portrayed a formidable power. In fact, however, the military stalemate along Ottoman frontiers in Europe continued in the early years of the century. The Ottoman Empire experienced severe internal difficulties, marked most vividly by the murder of Sultan Osman II in 1622. The fundamental institutions of the Empire were threatened in numerous ways: by a surge in population, and the inability of the economy to absorb the increase; by the decline of the *timar* system of land tenure, with deleterious effects on cultivation, law enforcement, and tax collection; and the growth of bitter and violent factionalism within the ruling class. Factions trying to usurp the Sultan's position, out to reap private gains within the system became more dangerous when the dynasty abandoned the practice of royal fratricide, upon the ascent of a new ruler. Rulers now let their brothers live, shut up in the harem. Sultan Ahmet I (1603-1617), a youth when he came to the throne, kept his brother Mustafa alive; he, though insane, ruled briefly in 1617 and again in 1622-1623 after the death of Sultan Osman. Harem women naturally became more powerful, and a vast, sometimes murderous politics of intrigue grew up around the ruler. Factions within the palace sought the aid of military units, with their own axes to grind. Soldiers could be accomplices or ringleaders; in 1622 they killed Sultan Osman.[4]

A good example of Ottoman troubles seen through English eyes is found in the report of Sir Henry Lello, ambassador from 1597 to 1607. Lello felt himself lost among barbarians and was glad to note their troubles. He compiled a long and colorless narrative of internal upheavals during the Ottoman-Habsburg war of 1593-1606. He allotted a section of his narrative to each Grand Vizir; it was the method of Knolles applied to the Vizirs rather than to the Sultans, and to internal troubles rather than foreign conquests. In Lello's eyes, the Grand Vizir was a "viceroy", usually at odds with the Mufti, a "general pope", and with Safiye, the grandmother of Sultan Ahmet I. He eventually banished her, but Lello saw eight Grand Vizirs destroyed by soldiers who hated the fact that they were often paid in worthless money. With the main army in Hungary, mutinies in the capital or in Anatolia were extremely dangerous. After one armed clash with rebels, the Sultan was forced to come to terms with them, first resolving "never again a soldier to be."[5]

Lello foresaw no immediate collapse. Strongmen like the Grand Vizir Kuyucu (Gravedigger) Murat Paşa (1606-1611) impressed him with their determination to end the war with Austria and crush rebels in Anatolia. The Ottoman Empire would survive its troubles, and in London, King James continued to worry. After Sultan Osman came to power in 1618, the

Ottomans mounted attacks in the Ukraine and in Poland. In England, late news was at hand:

> True copies of the insolent, cruell . . . letter lately written by the great Turke for denouncing of warre against the King of Poland, and of the answer made by the same King.

> News from Turkie and Poland, or a true and compendious declaration of the proceedings between the Great Turke and His Majesty of Poland, from the beginning of the warres untill the latter end.

King James was plainly worried. He told his ambassador in Istanbul, Sir Thomas Roe, that the Turks would now surely try to take advantage of Christian dissention, ". . . prosecuting those furious and violent ends which it seems he professeth by that great armie, wherewith he comes marching in person towards Christendom." Roe was to restrain the Sultan with "round Admonitions", but raise no threat of war, ". . . which at this time might prove dangerous to our subjects, and their fortunes, who have trade within his dominions."[6]

Following the death of Sultan Osman in 1622, Ottoman pressure everywhere subsided until the terrifying reformer Murat IV (1623-1640) mastered his capital and his household. Then, beginning in 1628, the Ottomans turned to the East, capturing Baghdad in 1638. Fighting in Hungary was sporadic, but in the Mediterranean the Ottomans attacked Crete in 1645.

One feature of English writings on the Turks in the early seventeenth century was the continuation of Knolles' narrative. For the edition of 1638 there were continuations by Edward Grimstone for 1609-17; a section on Osman II "out of the papers of Sir Thomas Roe and since by him reviewed and corrected"; and then Thomas Nabbes for the years 1628-1637, following Knolles' own "Briefe Discourse . . .". Both Grimston and Nabbes reproduced what they said were letters from diplomatic correspondence between London and Istanbul having mostly to do with the question of piracy; the section on Osman II will be considered below.

At the opposite extreme from the massive fifth edition of

Knolles were many sensational accounts of adventures throughout Ottoman Turkey and Safavid Iran, by land and sea, at court and in combat. One example, for the stage, was John Day's *The Travailles of the Three English Brothers* (1607), which played up the outlandish schemes of the Sherley brothers to divert Persian silk from Ottoman routes and ports. Anthony Nixon's *The Three English Brothers*, was a retelling of the tale.[7] More interesting were the adventures of Captain John Smith, a version of which appeared in 1630 with sequential drawings of Smith in "single combats"; the title told the whole story:

> . . . *Captain John Smith . . . His Accidents and Sea Fights in the Straights, His Service and Strategems of War . . . his three single combats betwixt the Christian armie and the Turkes. And how he was taken prisoner by the Turks, sold for a slave . . . how he slew the Bashaw . . . and escaped . . .*

Although chapter headings promised information on "Warres, Religion, and lawes," it was not to be found. Smith did mention a beverage, "coffa, boiled with water." He summed up his impressions of the Turks generally:

> For all their miserable knowledge, furniture and equipage, the mischief they do in Christendome is wonderfull, by reason of their hardness of life and constitution, obedience, agilitie, and their Emperour's bounty.[8]

The field of travel literature belonged to Samuel Purchas, who collected and popularized many travellers' journals and reports, in the tradition of Hakluyt.[9] The first edition of *Purchas his Pilgrimage* appeared in 1613, and there were many later editions. The great compilation appeared in 1625 under the title *Hakluytes Posthumus, or Purchas his Pilgrimes, Containing a History of the World, in Sea Voyages and Land Travels, by English men and others*. The title page portrayed the world lying open to English merchants and travellers, Purchas' "pilgrimes." In a world intended by God for "mutuell commerce", the English must be wary of their chief rivals, the Dutch, and deaf to calls for Crusades against the Turks. These came from Catholics and Anabaptists hoping to disrupt "mutuell commerce." There is no danger of a "Mahumetane" conquest of the world, and in the Ottoman Empire Christians maintain their heritage. The Turks do not spread religion by the sword.[10]

Purchas included an account by Sir Thomas Glover of his embassy in Istanbul, from 1607 to 1611. Glover meant mainly to justify Ambassador Edward Barton's journey to Hungary with the army of Sultan Mehmet III in 1596. Barton's presence in the camp of the Ottomans benefitted rather than harmed the cause of Christendom. Another Englishman in Hungary, however, did definite harm; Barton had told Glover about an English trumpeter who betrayed the town of Eger, slipping into Ottoman lines with information about the city's defences.[11]

There followed an account of travel in Eastern Anatolia, a region rarely visited by any Europeans. The author, William Biddulph, was the Company chaplain in Aleppo. He was often befriended by Anatolian nomads, the "Turcomanny." He found them to be

> kind and simple people dwelling alwayes in the fields, following their flockes, borne and brought up, living and dying in Tents . . . after the manner of the ancient Israelites . . . thee women keepe their Tents, and spend their time in spinning or carding . . . not spending their time in gossipping and gadding about . . . as many idle Huswives in England doe . . .[12]

He also described the preparation, social importance and physical benefits of coffee, a

> blacke kinde of drinke made of a Pulse like Pease called coava, which being ground in the Mill and boiled in water they drink it as hot as they can . . . It is accounted a great courtesee among them to give unto their friends when they come to visit a Fin-ion or Saidella of Coffe. . . . It causeth good concoction and driveth away drowsiness.[13]

Biddulph added a short glossary of Turkish salutations, as "Hosh Geldanos, Sophi Galdanos: that is, Welcome, my dear friend."

Yet in the end it was all Satanic, strange, and cruel. By the

Turks' worship of saints and dervishes, he wrote, one "may see how the Devill doth delude them still as hee did their Forefathers at the first by Mahomet's Machiavellian devices."[14] In the Ottoman Empire Jewish doctors murder Christian patients, and gruesome impalings were common. He was glad to be English:

> So many in England know not their own Felicitie . . . If they were here in this Heathen countrie they would know what it is to live in a Christian Commonwealth, under the government of a godly King, who ruleth by Law and not by lust . . . and God long continue his mercies to our noble King James.[15]

George Sandys' *A Relation of a Journey Begun An: Dom: 1610,* reprinted in Purchas, tried to analyze as well as describe the Ottoman Empire. Sandys visited Istanbul in 1610, and stayed for four months as guest of the Ambassador, Thomas Glover. His work went through six editions in English between 1615 and 1672, and by 1669 it had also appeared in Dutch and German. From time to time Sandys relieved his general hostility with an impartial or perceptive observation. Thus, while Islam is the creation of a mutinous and epileptic Byzantine soldier, a thoroughly false and devilish teaching, in the Ottoman Empire, "they compel no man."[16] The conquest of Chios was savage, "yet have the Christians their Churches, and unrepressed exercise of religion."[17] The Turks

> are a lazy people, that work but by fits . . . yet they are excessive covetous. . . . They have not the wit to deceive (for they be grosse-headed) yet they have the will, breaking all compacts with the Christians. . . .[18]

—Yet Turkish children are "the sweetest children that I ever saw."[19]
  In traveling the land, the visitor will find

> no Innes for entertainment throughout inhospitable Turkie . . . the Turks will receive your money and give you a quantity for it . . . rather exceeding than short of your expectations . . .[20]

54

Istanbul was a "Citie by destinie appointed and by nature seated for Sovereigntie . . . whose harbour is . . . throughout the world the fairest, safest and the most profitable."[21] Yet it was the capital of an Empire ruled by slaves. There is no nobility, but only the upstart creatures of the Sultan. His slaves are the nerves and supporters of the monarchy.[22] The monarch is lord over the greatest Empire in human history. "Hee that shall see 300,000 in an Armie (as he might have done this last Summer in Bithnyia) . . . should not wonder at their victories, but how the rest of the yet unvanquished world hath withstood them."[23]

Still, Sandys detected the first signs of stagnation and decay.

The body being grown too monstrous for the head, the Sultans unwarlike. . . . Empire so got, when it ceaseth to increase doth begin to diminish . . . It hath exceeded the observed period of a Tyranny. . . .[24]

Sultan Ahmet was an unknown quantity, apparently master of his court and household, builder of a great mosque at the Hippodrome, but still untested.[25]

Other visitors to Istanbul in the early years of the century included William Lithgow, Thomas Coryate, Peter Mundy, and George Gainsford. Lithgow, dour and hostile, was there in 1611. In 1614 he published *A most delectable and true discourse of an admired and painful Peregrination . . .* , which was reprinted later in 1632 as *The Rare Adventures of William Lithgow*. He recorded personal adventures but added little new to the image of the Ottoman Empire. He described the Battle of Lepanto, the "noble fields of Illium," and Istanbul—"Painted whore, the mask of deadly sin sweet faire without and stinking foule within."[26]

Coryate was in Istanbul in 1612 and 1613. A severely edited version of his notes appeared in 1625 in Purchas, revealing indiscrimately wide interests and containing vivid descriptions of what happened to catch his eye:[27] processions comparable to Roman triumphs, great fires, and fireflies, grasshoppers, and encounters with fortune tellers. He described the devotions of dervishes in Galata, "the strangest exercises of Devotion that ever I saw or heard of . . . a very ridiculous and foolish Musicke":

> They began by little and little to turne about the Interpreter of the Law
> turning gently in the middest of them all, afterward they redoubled their
> force, turned with such incredable swiftnesse, that I could not chuse but
> admire it. . . . . This turning they kept for the space of one whole houre at
> the least . . . with an acclamation of all the Turkes that stood by.[28]

Later, on the Prophet's birthday, he described "the most resplendent and glittering show":

> The Turkes hanged all their Turkish Mosquïes both of Constantinople
> and Galata with Lampes . . . a glorious red and refulgent spectacle. . . .
> Above all the rest of the Towers those foure that belong to the Temple of
> Solyman the magnificent made a most incomparable bright show.[29]

Peter Mundy visited Istanbul in 1617-1620. His works remained unpublished until modern times. For descriptions of Istanbul he referred readers to Sandys, and recommended also the work of Michel Baudier, translated into English in 1633.[30] He was interested in executions, which he described and illustrated in some detail, and public "entertainments" featuring swings "equalling the flight of a Bird in the Ayr" for adults, and ferris wheels for children.[31]

George Gainsford found nothing that he liked, a reaction not subtly hinted at in his title: *The Glory of England . . . with a Justifiable comparason betweene the eminent Kingdomes of the Earth and Herselfe: plainly manifesting the defects of them all* . . . In Istanbul he found no

> good lodging, proportionable fare, free recourse, gracious entertainment,
> true religion, secure abidement, allowable pleasure, or any thing wherein
> a noble citie is made glorious indeed. . . .

Much more informative and influential was Robert Withers' *The Grand Signor's Seraglio,* 1620. This book may have been a version or copy of an earlier work by Ottaviano Bon, who represented Venice in Istanbul from 1606 to 1609.[32] Purchas claimed that Withers knew Turkish, though it is difficult to see what use he may have made of it. He wrote as if he had had the run of Topkapi Saray, thanks to an Ottoman friend, the "Kahiya of the Bustangi Bashee" (steward of the Chief of the Gardeners; the *Bostanci-başi* was responsible also for policing the Palace).[33] He seemed familiar with the make-up and procedures of the Divan, the Imperial Council, and he knew of "the King's private awfull window looking into the Chamber."[34] Withers was most attentive to what he called "the carnall commerce with the King: He described the Harem as a harsh and closely regulated institution of "young, lusty, lascivious wenches." His title for this section was: "Of the Persons which live in the Seraglio and first of the Women and Virgins and their manner of life there." He also wrote vividly of the acquisition and training of Christian and Turkish youths in the palace schools:

> This Serraglio may rightly bee termed the Seminarie or Nurcerie of Subjects: for in it they have their bringing up, which afterward become the principall Officers . . . of the whole Empire.[35]

The discipline and curriculum are "nothing resembling the Barbarisme of Turkes, but beseeming subjects of singular Vertue and Discipline."[36]

When Withers turned to Islam, his tone was fair and free of diatribe. In all, his account was without rancor, but it was varied and dense. Long lists of officers, with their titles and functions in the Palace suggest an equerry's handbook. The atmosphere is oppressive, with eleven pages on the "King's" meals. Information of this kind might well have come from such a confidant as he claimed, "the Bustangee Bashee's steward." The "Bashee" himself was surely an important person,

> for hee steeres the King's Kaick and weareth a Turbent upon his head in the Serraglio, although he were but lately an Agiomoglan, and did wear one of the aforesaid felt Caps. . . .[37]

Withers' tone and style was echoed in 1633 in a translation of Michel Baudier's *Histoire générale du Serrail et de Court du Grand Seigneur*, 1624. Baudier's writings on Turkey have been characterized as purely descriptive, calculated to appeal to those interested in the exotic.[38] The English translation of 1633 carried the informative subtitle: *Wherein is seen the Image of the Ottoman Greatness. A table of humane passions, and the Example of the Inconstant Prosperities of the Court.* Baudier claimed as his source "a learned physician" to the Sultan; from him he learned of Constantinople, "the fatall abode of the most powerful Emperours of the Earth," sacked in 1453 in revenge for the destruction of Troy; and of the Palace, which he described in great and imaginative detail. In the Palace Christian youths are turned into Turks:

> The order and method wherewith they breed them up, doth testify that the Turks have retained nothing of the barbarous but the name, and have sent us the effect.[39]

A later edition contained a quintessential image of travel literature, a description of the Yedikule fortress:

> . . . Guedicular . . . the fort of the seven Towers, in which the wonders of Art was so great in old time, in what was spoken in the one was heard in all the rest successively and in order. . . . The one was full of Ingots and coyned gold; two of them contaned the silver that was coyned and in Ingots; another had diverse armes and ornaments for Souldiers and the Caparisons for Horses, enricht with gold, silver, and precious stones; the fifth served for ancient Armes, Medales and other precious remynders of Antiquity; the sixt contained the Engines for Warre, the seventh, the Rols and Records of the Empire.[40]

Before midcentury there were three more important depictions of the Ottoman Empire, stressing, in turn, Ottoman stability and power, the regicide of 1622, and the enlightening effects of travel.

Giovanni Botero emphasized Ottoman stability and power in *The Traveller's Breviat,* which appeared in 1630. He likened "the Great Turke" to the Emperor of Russia: both tyrants rather than true monarchs. He was most interested in the "Janiziers"

> . . . that carry the greatest fame throughout the Ottoman Empire both in the Field, the Court, and the City insomuch that the Sultans themselves have been afraid of their isolencie, yet tearme the Emperour Father (for no known friend besides have they to relie on) and hee again in time of war committeth his person to their trust, valour, and fidelity.[41]

The Ottomans "are Lords of three things, wherewith they terrifie the whole world: multitude of men unconquerable; military discipline (if so at this Day) uncorrupted; of Corne and provisions infinite".[42] Yet imperial expenses were surprizingly light: one million nine hundred three score and eight thousand seven hundred thirty five pounds nineteen shillings and eight pence sterling.[43] The disparity between available resources and current expenditures is explained by the Sultan's "timariots and stipendiaries by which he keeps the land in good cultivation", and

> maintaineth an hundred and fifty thousand horsemen, excellent well armed. . . . So great a Cavalry can no other Prince maintaine with the yearly expense of fourteen millions of gold . . . Herein consisteth the chiefest Preservation of the Ottoman Empire.[44]

The same, almost incredible point drew the attention of Thomas Nabbes, who continued Knolles' narrative for the period 1628-1637. It astounded English writers of the seventeenth century that the Ottoman Sultan should have, at no apparent cost, such an immense force.

> For no man can enjoy any possessions but he is enjoyned to entertain a certaine number of souldiers, proportionable to the revenues of the land . . . of these Timariots they are able to raise an hundred and fifty thousand horse . . . the Prince disburtheth not a Penny.[45]

The dramatic events in Istanbul in 1622 were just as astounding. No single event in Ottoman history drew more attention in England than the shocking overthrow and murder of Sultan

Osman II. Osman, an aggressive fighter and potential reformer was deposed and murdered shortly after the Janissaries broke into the Palace on May 19, 1622. He was replaced by his uncle, Mustafa, who had been deposed in favor of Osman in 1618 and would be deposed again in 1623. There were English pamphlets to keep readers informed: *A true and faithfull relation of what hath lately happened in Constantinople concerning the death of Sultan Osman and the setting up of Mustafa his uncle;* and *The Strangling and Death of the Greate Turke and his two sonnes. With the stranger Preservation and deliverance of his uncle Mustafa from perishing in prison.*

Purchas included a description "according to the Relation presented to His Majesty" that was almost identical with the version attributed to Thomas Roe in the fifth edition of Knolles (1638). Roe's papers did not appear under his name until 1740. Roe believed that the death of the Sultan poisoned the Ottoman state. In January 1622 he wrote:

> .... Your Lordship may behold in a dymme glasse our motions: fit matter for Ben Jonson. If I durst augure, I would, by these beastes entrails, that are daily butchered, pronounce the imminent ruine of this great monarchy, now, I think, yrrecouerably sick.[46]

Osman had had a bold plan to halt the decline of Ottoman power. Returning from his stalled campaign in Poland in 1621, the Sultan would then leave his capital for Anatolia, pretending to make a pilgrimage to Mecca. Roe thought he planned to raise an army in Eastern Anatolia, perhaps among the "Coords," "men ever bredd in the frontire hardnesse and warre, of great courage and experience." Then he would return to Istanbul in force and rid himself of the Janissaries.

> Certainly this was a brave and well grounded designe, and of great consequence for the renewing of this decayed Empire, languishing under the isolencies of lazy slaves, if God had not destroyed it . . .

A fatal flaw in the Sultan's character undid his plan. "He had one vice that resisted all hope of prosperity, which was extreme

60

avarice." His preparations for departing from Istanbul were not those of a devout and unencumbered pilgrim, but instead those of a greedy and laden-down ruler about to take flight. He gave himself away, and the results were gruesome. Roe described the butchery of the Sultan's vizirs, with some intimations of cannibalism, and the death of Osman: "a strong knaue stroke him on the head with a battle axe, and the rest, leaping upon him, strangled him with much adoe". Later Roe learned that, a month before his death, the Sultan had had a dream that foretold his fate but which he had not understood. He had asked a learned man to explain the dream; the man understood it instantly but, afraid to speak, sent the Sultan on to his imprisoned uncle, who did explain the portents to the ruler. The Sultan discounted them. Six days before the end, Roe himself, he said, tried in vain to persuade one of the Sultan's entourage to postpone the royal departure from Istanbul. Now, with Mustafa on the throne, "the ghost of Osman will not rest. . . . I am sure the whole body is sick. . ."[47] In May, 1623 he noted: ". . . there wants nothing butt some strong hand to push this tottering wall;"[48] by September of that year, he had seen the rise and fall of "three emperours, seaven great viziers, two capten bassas, five agas of the Janizaries, 3 treasorers, 6 bassas of Cairo" etc.[49] Rebels defied and confounded the government with laughable ease:

> . . . It is unresolved here how to proceed with Abassa bassa, who continueth to spoyle, or put to ransome Asya the Lesse, and cannot be reconciled for the Janizaryes, nor safely attempted for the Spahees, betweene which two Orders there is bad intelligence and emulations . . .[50]

In the Summer of 1624 the towns along the Bosporus were attacked by Cossacks, who burnt ships and houses along the channel to within four miles of Istanbul. To Roe, their success was new and welcome evidence of Ottoman weakness. In a ponderous, almost unmanageable allusion he noted

> how weak and unprovided they (the Turks) are. Just as the oracle commanded them (the Greek founders of the fishing village Byzans, i.e.,

Byzantium) first to seate over agaynst blind men (the inhabitants of Chalcedon, across the Bosphorus from Byzans) it hath bene their (the Turks') fortune to have to this day blynd enemyes (the rulers of Europe). Phillip of Macedon had never protected nor his sonne Alexander never adventured . . . if they had not discouered the effeminate faint courage of the Asiaticques . . .[51]

But the Ottoman Empire survived its most recent difficulties. Sultan Mustafa was quickly deposed, and Sultan Murat IV (1623-1640) began a long reign marked by internal reform and foreign conquest. Roe's reference to the "faint courage of Asiaticques," however, was typical of a growing tendency of English authors to make characterizations of the kind that would today be called national or ethnic stereotypes. Another early example of such labelling of the Turks, and others, was found in Henry Marsh, *A New Survey of the Turkish Empire and Government . . . with their Laws, Religion, and Customs* (1633). Later editions appeared in 1663 and 1664. The tone was extremely unpleasant. Throughout, the hardy Hungarians, the robust Germans, the quick French, the prudent Italians, the grave Spanish, and the valiant English are contrasted with the feeble Egyptians, the decadent Greeks, and the "inhumanly fierce" Scythian Turks. The only proper response to them was a Crusade:

For this Asian people, once the nauseated and basest dregs of the World, odious for their Luxury and infamous for their Slavery . . . are now by their temperance and abstemiousness (the Injunction and Discipline of an absurd Religion) become the mightiest Nation and greatest Lord of the Universe. . . .[52]

One final work from the first half of the century commands attention. Henry Blount's *Voyage into the Levant,* 1636, offered that author's impressions from a tour he began in 1634. By 1671 his work had gone through eight editions in English and one in German, and a Dutch version appeared in 1707.[53] Apart from its anti-Semitism, it set a new standard for fairness and impartiality in English travel literature.

Blount travelled to learn. The most certain and useful knowledge comes from travel abroad, away from the familiar "Christian institutions" of the West. The East and the West were sharply differentiated by religion, climate, and, most of all, by the Turks. They

were the only modern people great in Action. . . . He who would behold these times in their greatest glory could not find a better scene than Turkey. These considerations sent me thither, where my general purpose gave me four particular cares: first, to observe the religion, manners, and policies of the Turks . . . so far as might satisfy this scruple whether to an impartial conceit, the Turkish way appear absolutely barbarous . . . or another kind of civility, different from ours but no less pretending; secondly, in some measure to acquaint myself with those other sects which live under the Turks . . . especially the Jews, a race [which] remains obstinate, contemptible, and infamous; thirdly, to set the Turkish army then going against Poland. . . . ; last, . . . to view Grand Cairo . . . clearly the greatest concourse of mankind in these times, and perhaps that ever was. . . .[54]

With these ambitions, Blount left Venice for Spalato in 1634, on a Venetian ship. Her passengers included no Christian other than himself. Travelling overland in Dalmatia and on to Sarajevo, he encountered Turkish armies moving North, for Poland. He saw strict order and discipline, and severe punishment for looters. He talked with several officers, who tried to persuade him to turn Turk. Blount declined, but told them that his King was in league with the Sultan, and thought him the greatest monarch in the world. The English greatly admire Turkish accomplishments, he went on, and they appreciate the "kinde Commerce of Trade we find amongst them."[55] After ten days at Edirne, where he visited the Selimiye mosque, Blount finally reached Istanbul. He had been *en route* for fifty two days. His guide, a Janissary, had remained in Edirne, choosing not to risk active service by being seen in the capital.[56] He stayed in Istanbul only five days before sailing to Alexandria. "The strangest thing I found among the Turkish mariners," he wrote, "was their incredable civilitie. . . ."[57]

Blount described the Ottoman conquest of Egypt and their

subsequent legal reforms as enthusiastically as he did the Pyramids. Ottoman law made travel safe.[58]

After briefly describing his return to Europe, the *Voyage into the Levant* becomes an analysis of the Ottoman Empire. Not to be thought hasty and superficial, Blount argued that his quick glance took in all the eminent features. It is the passing eye rather than the steady gaze that best appreciates scarlet. The judgment of a newcomer is fresh and sincere, whereas familiarity corrupts with affection or hatred. He would judge the Ottoman Empire only by its major institutions: the army, religion, justice, and "moral customes."[59] He claimed as source some Ottoman soldiers, anxious to befriend and impress him. Blount was most interested in the Janissaries. They bore the inherited traditions of Greek and Roman discipline, together with the Turkish emphasis upon rewarding merit. He recommended this to the states of Christendom. Yet the old discipline was waning, partly because Turks were now enrolled in the Corps, but also because the Janissaries had lost forever their age-old discipline when they shed the blood of Sultan Osman in 1622. The monarchy was the keystone, and the "foundation of all monarchy, that is due awe toward the Blood Royal."[60]

Blount had nothing favorable to say about Islam, describing it as "daintie fruit growing out of a Dung Hill." But his attitude towards all faiths was deeply and, for his time, unusually skeptical: " . . . the vertues of vulgar minds are of so base a nature as must bee manured with foolish hopes and fears, as being too grosse for the finer instruments of reason." He went on to say that the Turks interpret the Koran literally, and made religion suit the needs of the state. Their lands do not lie dead in the grasp of the clergy.[61]

Ottoman justice differed markedly from Christian practice. He saw it as quick, severe, and arbitrary. Judges decided cases with the needs of the state foremost in mind. To maintain and augment power required that the ruler make the laws conform to the conscious purposes of the state. Thus Sultan Murat IV paid the soldiers regularly, and scrupulously maintained the privileges of merchants and other visitors.[62] Christians lacking the protection of an ambassador or a capitulary agreement might be seized and sold into slavery, but on the whole Turkish rule was not tyrannical. The Sultan does not rule through strangers or mercenaries, but is maintained by his own subjects. He seems a tyrant, but the Janissaries may rise against him at any moment. Much depended on the personality of the ruler; Murat IV had little to fear from any man.

By "moral customes" Blount meant spiritual qualities. These he found reflected in the nature of the Ottoman state, made great by the spiritual "metal" of its founders and their successors. Nature intended none to rule, nor none to suffer bondage. The Turks created the power that brings the world to its knees; situated between Persia and Christendom, they are the vigilant enemies of all. Their institutions and demeanor reflect that vigilance. They are disdainful of foreigners and their ways. It is, however, the furthest thing from barbarism. Instead, the Ottoman Empire is a model of social and political conservatism.[63]

"Thus," said Blount,

I have set down what I noted in the Turkish customs; all instruct, either by error or imitation; Nor is the mind of Man a Perfect Paradise, unless there be planted in it the Tree of Knowledge, both of Good, and Evill.[64]

5

"To Imitate The Sun"—The Present State of The Ottoman Empire

The reign of Sultan Murat IV (1623-1640) restored stability to the Ottoman Empire. Episodes of instability before 1623 had stimulated English interest; now it was evident that these episodes were not fatal to the Ottoman Empire. With Murat's death, however, the internal weaknesses of the Empire became apparent again, in a new time of troubles. The English perception of the Ottomans, meanwhile, was somewhat unstable itself, reflecting political changes in London as well as in Istanbul. After 1640, political upheavals threatened to alter the character of both England and the Ottoman Empire. Rebellions in Anatolia were coincident with the Civil War in England. Sultan Ibrahim (1640-1648) fell to the executioner in 1648, and Charles I was executed in 1649. When Paul Rycaut came to Istanbul in 1661 as the Ambassador's secretary, he wrote that the history of the turbulent years just before his arrival enabled him to "understand how King Charles the Glorious Martyr was put to death."[1] At mid-century political power in both states was in new hands. Charles Stuart was absent until his Restoration in 1660, and Mehmet IV (1648-1687) was leaving most decisions to his capable Grand Vizirs, Mehmet Köprülü (1656-1661) and his son Ahmet (1661-1676). Throughout the period English writers were comparing events in England and Turkey. The writer of one pamphlet recorded an imaginary conversation between Charles I and Ibrahim.[2] A pamphlet by "R.M.", *Learne of a Turke: or instructions and advice sent from the Turkish Army at Constantinople to the British Army at London* described the overthrow of Sultan Osman, compared it with the execution of Charles I, and demanded the restoration of Charles II.[3] Paul Rycaut described Sultan Mehmet's hatred for Istanbul; his return to that city in 1665 after a long absence reminded Rycaut' of Charles II's return to London in 1660; "The humour which then possessed Constantinople," he said, "appeared like that of London at the King's Restoration; all joy, even to transport, for this unexpected return. . . ."[4]

Francis Osborne's *Political Reflections on the Government of the Turks* (1656) was written in the same spirit of comparison, but criticized the Stuarts and the Catholic monarchs of Europe. Osborne admired the Ottoman practice of subjecting ecclesiastical power to civil power. The Ottoman state was no more brutal and tyrannical than the monarchies of Europe. With the Ottomans, power depends upon merit rather than birth; hence the Ottomans are free from corruption and idleness, the ruination of Christianity.[5] Other Ottoman "maxims" included the unity of political and military power in the Sultan, strict limits on the numbers of office-holders and other functionaries, and constant warfare to keep the soldiers from standing idle. Osborne concluded with an invidious comparison between the standards of the Ottoman court and those of the Catholic monarchs of Europe.[6] His work would have been of little use to any reader trying to grasp Ottoman realities at mid-century, but it was published often, in 1672, 1673, 1689, 1697, 1701 and 1719. It is difficult to say whether readers were more attracted by a brief analysis of the Ottoman Empire or by a timely critique of monarchy.

The most enduring nexus of contact between England and the Ottoman Empire remained trade. The Ottomans renewed the English Capitulations seven times during the century, for the last time in 1675. English exports in cloths, lead, and tin were the basis of their favorably balanced trade in raw silk throughout the first half of the century. Trade fell off during the years of the Civil War and the Protectorate, but improved after the Restoration. The King granted The Levant Company a new charter in

1661, and English writers attributed the improvement also to the policies of the Köprülü Grand Vizirs, Mehmet and Ahmet.[7]

Mehmet Köprülü came to power in the midst of a severe military emergency in 1656, when Istanbul was in danger of a Venetian naval attack. He was an outstanding example of an individual's rise from obscure and humble origins, through the slave system, to a position of great power. Before taking office he set conditions: that his orders, when submitted to the Sultan for approval, be executed without question; that he have absolute power of appointment and absolute freedom of action in political and military matters; and, finally, that the Sultan ignore whatever intrigues his many enemies might mount against him. The conditions were accepted, and Mehmet Köprülü, then 81, accepted the signet ring on August 14, 1656.

Köprülü solved the Empire's most immediate problem in 1657, recapturing the islands Lemnos and Tenedos from Venice, securing Istanbul from attack. He launched a heavy-handed program of internal reform, based on the belief that corruption and graft were the real enemies of traditional Ottoman statecraft. To eliminate them, he established a reign of terror. The number of victims has been variously estimated from 30,000 to 400,000. He also won the Sultan's assurance that he would be succeeded by his son Ahmet; Ahmet's appointment in 1661 was a definite break with Ottoman custom.

Both vizirs attempted to make new conquests in the West. Mehmet Köprülü built a powerful fortress at the site of ancient Abydos in 1659, and also mounted an invasion of Transylvania. Though defeated by the Habsburgs at St. Gothard on the Raab in 1664, Ahmet Köprülü's armies had fought well and remained intact. The Grand Vizir achieved his objective in Transylvania and Hungary in the Treaty of Vasvar; Crete and Poland remained targets. The siege of Candia in Crete continued until its surrender in 1669. An invasion of Poland in 1676 led to Ottoman suzerainty over the Ukraine.[8]

English trade during all this did very well, reaching a peak between 1666 and 1683. Prosperity rested again on the exchange of cloths for silk. The yearly volume of cloths sold was between

15 and 16 thousand pieces. In fact, since the Ottomans did not permit specie to be taken out of the Empire until after 1680, the English faced a problem in procuring enough silk to pay for the great quantity of cloths sold; the expansion of cloth exports to the Ottoman Empire simply outran the Ottoman ability to supply raw silk. Other products had to be found to fill the gap. These included cotton from western Anatolia, shipped from Izmir; (Izmir was the location of the largest English community in Turkey after 1675); mohair yarn, galls for dyes and inks, dried fruit, again loaded at Izmir; goat and camel hair; carpets, dyes, drugs and coffee, all in small quantities. England imported coffee also, from Egypt. Finally, the shipment of war materiel from England to Turkey continued. 250 naval guns were unloaded in 1654. Paul Rycaut acknowledged that "not three English miles from Vienna many poor people have been surprized and fallen into the hands of the Tartar and Turk", but noted that from the English trade with the Ottoman Empire ". . . his Majesty without any expense gains a very considerable increase in his Customs."[9]

If commerce was paramount, religion receded as a rewarding perspective on the Ottoman Empire. In 1656 Isaac Barrow, the teacher of Newton, described Islam in a fair-minded way, though he did include some elements of caricature. His *Epitome fidei et religionis turcicae*, in five parts, described the veneration of the Koran, the one-ness and omniscience of God (he "sees the footprint of a black ant on a black rock"; without his will "the wings of a fly" cannot move); the angels, especially Gabriel and Esrail; the divine authorship of the Bible and the Koran; and finally the prophets, from Adam to Muhammad.[10] Barrow was neither polemical nor condescending. In general, strident denunciations of Islam became rare, and many who wrote with religion in mind thought mostly of Greek Orthodoxy or Quakerism. Interest in the state of the Greek Church was an important consideration in the rise of neo-Hellenism in England, while for the Embassy in Istanbul, the relations between the Greek Church and "Popery" in Jerusalem became a vexing problem.[11]

English Quakers continued to believe that the Ottomans

would welcome and respond to the efforts of their missionaries. One, Mary Fisher, travelled to Turkey in 1657 to bring to Mehmet IV a statement of faith. The Earl of Winchelsea, Ambassador from 1661 to 1668, tried to prevent her journey, but she had an audience with Mehmet Köprülü, who referred her to the Sultan. The audience opened with a long period of silence, as she waited for the divine spark or light. When she did speak, the ruler, who was only sixteen, listened politely, thanked her for coming, and offered her an escort for her trip from Edirne to Istanbul, from where she might return to England. She preferred, however, to travel alone, and departed. Later she described the encounter:

> . . . he was very noble unto me. . . . There is a Royall seed amongst them, which in time God will raise. They are more Truthfull than many other nations . . . though they be called Turkes . . . They would willingly have me stay in ye country and when they could not . . . they proffered me a man and a horse to go five days journey that was to Constantinople.[12]

In 1661 one John the Quaker preached in the streets of Istanbul, in English, until handed over to the Embassy. Two works exhorting Quakers to follow in the footsteps of Mary Fisher and John were John Perrot's *A Visitation of love, and gentle greeting of the Turk. . . .* (1658) and his *Blessed Openings of a day of good things to the Turks (1661).*[13]

Travellers' images, vital and vivid, remained in good supply. John Burbury's travel journal is an excellent example of the genre. He travelled to Istanbul in 1664, stopping over in Belgrade and Edirne. Before he reached Istanbul he had witnessed an exchange of ambassadors (*mubadele*) at the Ottoman-Habsburg frontier, seen Mehmet IV, become acquainted with a physician and some soldiers he claimed as sources of information, and found time for reflecting and writing. *A Relation of the Journey of the Right Honourable My Lord Henry Howell from London to Vienna and thence to Constantinople* appeared in 1671. What information Burbury may have gained from his sources is unclear; the real value of his book lies in its descriptions of what he saw. Burbury and Howell travelled in the company of the Habsburg *Resident* Count Lesley. After describing the ceremonious passage of the Habsburg *Resident* and an Ottoman convoy into the territory of the other, he noted the escort that went on with his party:

> The Janissaries look stout fellows . . . , but the Horse had little and loose Necks and went tossing up their noses like Camels in the Air, and the Turks ride so short as 'tis a Kind of wonder, to see how they can run so easily about and with their halfpikes in their hands, cling so fast to their little and so uneasie Saddles.

The Janissaries that he had seen were better armed than English soldiers yet were "civil and courteous."[14] He also heard what must have been the *Mehter* music of the Janissary Corps:

> The Turks were strangely pleased with the Ambassador's Musick, both the vocal and the instrumental, and indeed they had reason, for their's is the worst in the world . . . It was like Tom a Bedlam, only a little sweetened with a Portugal like Mimikry. And the Musick most esteemed among the Souldiery is the shrillest and squeakiest Trumpet that was ever heard, and a bagpipe like instrument such as accompanies the Jackanapes to the Bear Garden, and other ill pipes and hoboys. . . .[15]

The voices of the *muezzins* were even worse; Burbury believed that *muezzins* substituted for clocks.

In Belgrade Burbury listened to the complaints of a local merchant dissatisfied with Turkish rule, but found in general that the Sultan's Christian subjects were rarely imposed upon. He was sure that the Sultan's subjects were not slaves. He noted many examples of religious toleration, and the Turks' scrupulous observance of the English trade agreements.[16] Still, he longed for Christendom and was glad at Niş to get mail from home. Further on, in Edirne, he witnessed the meeting between the "Ambassadour of the Emperour of the West and the Monarch of the East." Throughout his journey his hosts were hospitable, and fond of wine. They were born soldiers, kind to animals, and illiterate. But he had no high regard for Ottoman arms, or for Istanbul.[17]

William Seaman was both an observer and a minor participant in the affairs of the English in Turkey. He travelled to Istanbul in the service of Sir Peter Wyche, Ambassador from 1628 to 1639. He lived in the Embassy, and learned Turkish. The Ambassador's son, Cyril Wyche, became his patron (as, later, Robert Boyle did). His first work, published in 1652, was a purported translation of the Turkish chronicle of Hoca Saddudin Efendi (1536-1599), which he titled *The Reign of Sultan Orchan* and dedicated to Lady Jane Merrick, wife of the Ambassador. Saddudin was the *şeyhülislam* (chief jurisconsult) under Murat III (1574-1595) and then the teacher of Mehmet III (1595-1603). Saddudin's *Crown of Histories* covered the reigns of the Sultans through Selim I (1512-1520). Seaman's volume had the merit at least of pointing out the value of Ottoman sources. It was, he said, a specimen of what could be done in this kind; Knolles' "painfull" book was wrong to discount Turkish sources. In fact, ". . . there had not been then made that diligent inquisition, either to the elegancie of their language, as to know what they said . . ." Seaman wrote that he knew enough Turkish to define the essential terminology. "Islam" is the submission to the will of God, and to the religion instituted by the Prophet Muhammad. For "kuffar" (sic), the Turkish *kâfir* (unbeliever) Seaman felt obliged *not* to convey the correct meaning of unbeliever, or he who denies, but instead the devotion of Christians under Ottoman rule to the true faith, and their rejection of the false prophet Muhammad.[18]

His narrative comprised four themes: the sieges and battles of Sultan "Orchan" (Orhan), the exaltation of his royal dignity, the spread of Islam, and the establishment of law. The style is clear, with literary embelishments. In one such, "A relation of the taking of the castle of Aydos", the castle falls to the Turkish general "Abdyrahman" because of a dream and a romance. During the siege, a lady-in-waiting to the garrison commander's daughter suffered a terrifying dream, in which she was finally rescued from undescribed horrors by a heroic figure unknown to

73

her. When he appeared again, in the real world, she recognized him from the walls of the castle as the Turkish commander, Abdyrahman. She threw him a message, in Greek, which landed at his feet, telling him of her desire to turn to his faith, and also of how he might best take the castle. The plan was a success, and so was their marriage. Their child was

> called by the name of black Abdyrahman who arrived to such a degree of valour that the unbelievers of Constantinople for the terrour of him were restlesse, and sleep was forbidden their eyes, and mothers for the name of black Abdyrahman were wont to still their children.

As the narrative went on, Seaman stressed the zeal of "the army of Islam," the proximity to it of Constantinople, and the Turks' administrative skills. Orhan established a mint, collected children periodically as tribute, and maintained a uniformed and well organized army.[19] He divided his conquests into "bassaliks" ruled by "sanjak beghs" responsible to him in time of war for the number of horsemen proportionate to their revenues.[20]

Seaman concluded with a "commemoration of the Learned Men and among them of the Shichs which were in the time of Orchans reign." It was a rather disspassionate attempt to outline the hierarchy of the Ottoman *ulema*. The term was Arabic, and the hierarchy included all the learned Muslims within the Empire. The hierarchy administered both civil and divine law. Its fundamental distinction was between those bearing the title *mula*, signifying a judge, or doctor of law, and *shich*, the head of a dervish order.[21] Although he omitted the jurisconsults, or *mufti*, his account was more accurate and informative than anything which had preceded it. It bore little resemblance, however, to the religious establishment of the frontier society of Sultan Orhan.

Seaman succeeded in showing that what he referred to as "Master Knolles his Method" was not a timeless one. The use of Turkish sources was at least no longer inconceivable. Seaman's later work—a Turkish version of the *Book of John* (1659), a Turkish New Testament (1888), and a *Grammatica*

74

linguae turcicae (1670) showed that the Turkish language could become an important element in Turkish studies, and demonstrated the importance of basing Turkish studies on Turkish sources.

The prospect of such study was distant, however, and even receding. For one thing, the transaction of business seemed to encourage the prevailing, if varying, degrees of hostility, incomprehension, and condescension. John Finch, Ambassador from 1672 to 1681, wrote:

> I am sensible enough that all business of moment is hardly done, but here the perplexity of doing affairs is still attended with more difficulty and intrigue, by having to do with a people who neither in language, manners nor religion have any affinity with us.[22]

Published writing, therefore, tended to recapitulate the method and concerns of Knolles, in spite of Seaman's complaint. It displayed assiduous attention to detail and industrious effort to update political history, but within a generally accepted frame of reference. It was as if a canon had been established.

The most important writing came from those associated with The Levant Company; of these, Paul Rycaut's works stand out as those of a merchant, a traveller and a historian.

Rycaut was born in 1608 at Aylesford in Kent, the eighth son of Sir Peter Rycaut. Peter's father had been a Brabant merchant; Peter himself had come to England in the reign of James I and made a fortune in trade. He was knighted in 1641 but was ruined with the Cavalier defeat in the Civil War. He was barely able to send Paul to Trinity College, Cambridge, where the young man received his B.A. in 1650. He read law for a brief time, travelled to Italy and Spain, and resided at the Court of Charles II in Brussels. There he attracted the attention of Heneage Finch, second Earl of Winchelsea, whose secretary he became. Winchelsea, as a supporter of Charles II, became Ambassador in Istanbul in 1661, and it was as the Ambassador's secretary that Paul Rycaut went to Turkey in that year. From 1661 to 1667 he was also secretary of The Levant Company. In 1677 he became consul in Izmir. In 1666 he published the work which made him famous: *The Present State of the Ottoman Empire*. It went through twelve English editions, fourteen French, four Italian, three German, two Dutch, and one edition each in Polish and Russian.

The corpus of his works on the Ottoman Empire alone is immense, beginning with an anonymous account of his initial voyage to Istanbul and the reception in the Ottoman capital. In 1663 he published a copy of the new English Capitulations. *The Present State*, when it appeared in 1666, earned him election in the recently established Royal Society. In 1669 he wrote a short piece on Sabbatai Sevi, a messianic Jewish leader active in Izmir in 1665 and 1666. In 1679 he published copies of the renewed Capitulations. In 1679 he completed *The Present State of the Greek and Armenian Churches Anno Christi 1678*, and in 1679 his narrative history of the Ottoman Empire began to appear, with the first volume entitled *The History of the Turkish Empire from the Year 1623 to the Year 1677*. The second volume, *The Turkish History . . . with a Continuation by Sir P. Rycaut* appeared in 1687. The third, *The History of the Turks Beginning with the Year 1679 . . . until the End of the Years 1698 and 1699* was published in 1700, the year of Rycaut's death. An abridgement of the three volumes appeared in the following year.[23]

In the Introductory section of *The Turkish History* of 1687 Rycaut suggested a pattern for his vast work. At first he bridged the gap between the end of Knolles' continuations, in 1623, to 1640. For that, he relied on "Venetian sources." For his subsequent work, until his departure from Turkey in 1678, he suggested the comprehensive title of "Memoirs." After he left Turkey he continued his work from afar while a Levant Company director, Chief Secretary in Ireland, and English Resident in Hamburg and the Hansa towns.

Some of his earliest writing on Turkey came from a journey he made from Istanbul to London in 1663. He described one segment of the trip in a letter to Winchelsea:

That night I tooke a more knowing guide to conduct me over a mountaine . . . usually frequented with robbers, very steep in many places and rocky, and such narrow and difficult passages. . . . Neere the top the mountaine beganne to bee exceedingly pleasant, the highest point being a green'plaine with trees even and equally planted; the prospect of the country on the one side and of the sea on the other, the prodigious precipices and the delightful confusion of the rocks appearing with the dim light of the moone and the silence of the night rendered everything there a most pleasing object of the eye.

Later, near Gallipoli,

. . . the Caddie [*kadi*, judge] with much cavility provided me with provisions and attendants, and the governor sent me six lusty muske-teers . . . but the melancholy of the groves and quietnesse of the night beganne again to renew the sadnesse with which I parted from your lordship.

He sailed for England bearing a horse and scimitar, gifts from Winchelsea to the King. He later wrote that the King was

highly delighted with the horse, for I tooke such good care of him, to get him into good condition, that he looked as well in St James's Park . . . as he did at Adrianople . . . The horse is ordered to be sent to Newmarket, for the King hath a great opinion that he is very fleet.[24]

Something of Rycaut's character is shown by these letters to his master and patron, which was not so obvious and would be out of place in his historical writings. He appears to be preeminently a "man of sentiment" as well as a "man of the world"; the admiration for the quiet grandeur of nature and his love of the exotic make him seem almost an early romantic of a century later.

Rycaut's historical narrative begins with the year 1623, a time when the very survival of the Ottoman Empire was in doubt. Then

all things looked with that black appearance that nothing seemed to keep the frame of Empire together. . . . One would have imagined that Christian Princes would have seen their own interests and made use of the advantage, but God not having as yet fixed a Period to the Bounds of this Empire was pleased by His Secret Providence to divert both the Emperour and the King of Poland. . . .

From that miraculous respite emerged the conquering tyrant, Sultan Murat IV. Rycaut's description of his successful siege of Baghdad in 1638 still makes good reading. Then we have Murat as tyrant:

> Murat growing now into years, took unto his own Hands the Reins of Government, resolving to rule Singly and Absolutely, and to make himself rather Feared than Beloved.
> He was certainly the most absolute Prince that every swayed the Ottoman Empire . . . but of no Religion . . . [and] so great a Tyrant that at length he became his own Assassin.

The Sultan's creatures were men like himself—at first merely cruel and bestial, they became insolent and seditious. Murat's tyranny led to the regicide of Ibrahim in 1648, and a piling up of "malignant humours", the fevers, and the convulsions of a cruel internal struggle between the "spahees", whom Rycaut likened to a gentry, and the Janissaries. By 1656 the Empire was a scene of horror and confusion: "Merchants and well meaning citizens remained in the most astonishing apprehension imaginable."[25]

The Emperor's savior was "Kuperlee (that is, Mehmet Köprülü), Grand Vizir from 1656 to 1661. Rycaut saw him as antidote to the "great distempers of the State," and other observers, such as Isaac Barrow, agreed. Barrow, writing in 1658, thought that "Christendome seems likely to find its worst enemy in this man so bitterly intent on advancing Ottoman power." Rycaut, on the other hand, emphasized the renewal of good government, speaking of "bright beams."[26]

Five years after Köprülü came to power, Rycaut arrived in Istanbul. By 1666 he had completed *The Present State of the Ottoman Empire*. He intended it as a "true System or Model of the Turkish Government and Religion," a handbook for "Kings and Emperours" containing "the maxims of the Turkish politie," the "most material points of the Mahometan religion," and the Turks' "military discipline." He saw great need for the work, for

> . . . we contract prejudice from ignorance and want of familiarity. . . . A people, as the Turks are, men of the same composition with us, cannot be so savage and rude as they are generally described for ignorance and grossness is the effect of Poverty, not incident to happy men whose spirits are elevated with Spoils of so many Nations. . . .[27]

The Present State. . . . is an arcanum of disparate information, sensational tales, and elaborate computation, all giving an impression of definitiveness; but it is highly mannered, and the veneer of enlightened inquiry is patchy. The author's sources are touted but not precisely or convincingly defined. He claimed to have documents from the Embassy, registers and records from Ottoman vizirs and, on religious matters, from "learned doctors." Somewhat more specifically, he cited the help of an "understanding Polonian" who had spent nineteen years in the Ottoman court. Perhaps this was Albert Bobowski or Bobovius. He was captured in Poland and educated in the Palace, and served in the translator's bureau.[28]

Sources aside, Rycaut emphasized Ottoman "Tyranny, Oppression, and Cruelty" and advised the reader to "make thy Happiness breed thy Content without degenerating into wantonness or desire of revolution."[29] The horror of turmoil is driven home early with scenes of atheism, mutilations, stranglings, and cannibalism in the Palace. Thus, in the "True relation of the designs managed by the Old Queen . . . against her grandchild Sultan Mahomet," we read of the Queen's death:

> . . . the young officers found themselves unprovided of a Cord to strangle her, so that crying out for a Cord, one ran to the Royal Chappel, and thence took the Cord that upheld the great Antiport of the Mosch, which being turned about the Queen's neck, the aforesaid Dogangi, getting upon her back, pitched her neck with his hands, whilst the others drew the Cord. The Queen . . . above 80 years old and without Teeth . . . with her gumms only did bite the thumb of his left hand . . . until with the haft of his ponyard struck her on the fore-head near her right eye . . . The

> Queen raised herself, . . . the Cord was a second time applyed, and wrung so hard with the haft of a hatchet. . . .

and so on in revolting detail. Rycaut saw in this a lesson:

> . . . Arms can never be prosperous under the ensign and Conduct of a Usurper. And may all Christians learn this lesson from the Turks. . . . None can more experimentally preach this Doctrine to the World than England.[30]

Rycaut then turned his attention to the Ottoman state, likening all states to ships at sea which steer by certain immutable fixings, their "maxims." The Ottoman ship sailed a course so unique and irrational that it defied any conventional charting. One might suppose that

> the divine will of the all knowing Creator had chosen for the good of his Church and chastisement of the sins and vices of Christians to raise and support this potent People.

In fact, however, the Ottoman course proceeded directly from the Turks' Scythian origins, and perpetual war-mongering. These reinforce "the absoluteness of an Emperour without reason, without virtue." Tyranny is the natural condition of the Ottoman state. The Turkish ruler is no "just monarch;" he is unbound by law, and his Empire is a "fabrick of slavery," a "painted and shining servitude" with a "squalid, sordid, and noisome nature." It presents the grotesque spectacle of the rule of slaves, "it being a Maxim of the Turkish Policy to have the Prince served by such whom he can raise without Envy and destroy without Danger."[31] The Palace School shaped such men, instilling in them a hatred of their Christian parents and birthright, and compelling their unquestioning obedience. The curriculum included Arabic, Persian, Turkish, physical training, and "the accomplishment of a Trade, handycraft or Mystery, in which a man may be useful to the service of the Grand Signior." Those who emerged from the School into officialdom knew "the Ottoman way":

80

For the Turks, out of Pride and Scorn, comport themselves to Christians with a strange kind of barbarous haughtiness and neglect, they are yet among themselves as courtly and precise in their own rules of compliment and civility as they are at Rome or any other parts of the civilized world.[32]

The Ottomans knew nothing of the outside world, although

... as to the successes and progresses of Affairs in their own Dominions they keep most strict Registers and Records which serve them as presedents and rules for the present government.[33]

Yet beneath all lay the rotten core. In the School Rycaut detected 'the libidinous flame of depraved nature . . . so common a disease amongst the Turks," but poorly masked as "Platonick love." The black and white eunuchs are abhorrent symbols of ancient vice, now common in the "courts of Eastern Princes." The black, in particular, were in the image of Caliban: "They are not only castrated, but Black . . . , chosen with the worst features that are to be found among the most hard favoured of that African Race."[34]

Rycaut had little to say about the *harem*, describing only the preparations undergone by those chosen to visit the ruler. Lists of functionaries did for the rest of the "Seraglio", which he termed "one of the most Politick Constitutions in the World."[35] It must somehow have enabled the Empire to survive the violent and unstable days of the early seventeenth century. In a broader discussion of the "Turkish Government" Rycaut furnished additional lists of offices and provinces and information on Ottoman vassal states. He stressed the previous instability of all officers, particularly grand viziers. It was government as theater:

Fortune so strangely sports with this people that a Comedy or Tragedy on the stage with all its scenes is scarce sooner opened and ended, than the fate of divers great men, who in the daytime being exalted to high sublimity by the powerful rayes of the Sultan's favours, in the night fall, or vanish like a Meteor. The Grand Signior, to imitate the Sun, benights some parts of the world to enlighten others, so that by a general influence and communication of his Beams, he may be acknowledged the common Parent of them all.[36]

The overall impression Rycaut gives is of a highly organized but grotesque monolith, in which personal security is nonexistent but political stability is guaranteed. The well trained imperial administration was efficient and flexible. Provinces were administered variously, out of either local or imperial revenues. To compensate for the child tribute, now largely abandoned, the Ottomans made good use of apostates, from the "stupid ignorance of the Green and Armenian churches," and of the thousands of slaves taken for them by their "jackals," the "Tartars." Their raids in 1663 alone netted 160,000 slaves:

> they rob, burn, spoil, and carry all the inhibitants of what Age and Sex soever . . . like a torrent . . . a running march day and night . . . too fast for an orderly army to overtake . . .[37]

Government by desolation, depopulation, forced migration, confiscation, execution, imprisonment, elimination of all lines of hereditary succession (except in the Arab lands and Kurdistan,) make up Ottoman government. It is a machine known previously only in the pages of Machiavelli:

> this saith Machiavel . . . and the Turk understands . . . to use evil instruments . . .[38]

The relationship between Turks and Christians in the Ottoman Empire is unilateral: the Turks long ago sacrificed the purity of their "Saracen blood" by persuading their subjects to accept their God. They do everything in their power to weaken Christianity. "Considering the stupid ignorance in the Greek and Armenian Churches, the conservation of their faith is not to be attributed to anything more than to the strict observations of the Feasts and Fasts". Often, the Turks' outlandish attire was enough to attract Greeks and Armenians to Islam.[39] Rycaut did not mention the *millet* system, i.e., the Ottoman practice of ruling indirectly over the religious communities that made up the

82

Empire, allowing for religious toleration. As for those Christian ambassadors sent to them, the Turks recognized embassies as "sacred and necessary," but in time of war might take them hostage. The English, however, have nothing to fear. Their only weakness was in not knowing Turkish. Reason, courage and forthrightness go only so far with the Turks. Presents too have their place, but major efforts should be made to teach Englishmen Turkish.[40]

The second section of *The Present State* was devoted to Islam. A false religion, it easily beguiled the dull and unlearned with

gross conceptions of the beauty of women with great eyes, of the duration of one act of carnal Copulation for the space of sixty years . . .

The Ottomans claimed a divine mandate;

and the same argument (if I am not mistaken) in the time of the late Rebellion in England was made use of by many, to intitle God to their cause and make him the Author of their thriving sin.[41]

The subject which most interested Rycaut, however, was "the difference of the Sects, and disagreement in religion amongst the Turks in General." The division between the Turks, followers of "Mahomet", and the Persians, followers of "Hali" (Ali, son-in-law of the Prophet) constituted the fundamental division in Islam. Superstition once divided divides endlessly. Thus there appeared a vast number of sects, this one "purely Pythagorical," that one "purely Platonicall," and a third "may rather be termed the Sect of Epicureans. . . . Their monasteries and orders [provide] pretended mortification and strictness of life," but were in fact dens, offering liquor, opium, and sodomy. Rycaut explained that Mehmet Köprülü aimed to reduce their numbers and break their influence, if necessary by killing their inhabitants. He was more hostile and carping here than in perhaps any other part of his book; his account lacked the saving features of Coryat's description of "Ethnicke Devotion." By "sects" Rycaut meant the popular mystical orders following a prescribed path (*tarikat*) to union with God. He did not realize their importance in folk Islam, and the unifying, stabilizing role they played in Turkish life.[42] He was on more solid ground in enumerating and explaining "the five necessary points which are required to constitute a true Mahometan." He discussed "their washings", prayers, "Ramazan", "zacat", i.e., alms giving, and the pilgrimage. All were based on a profession of complete monotheism.[42]

Had Christianity anything to learn from Islam? Very little, Rycaut thought. But he did note the vast sums set aside in the Ottoman Empire for the endowment of mosques and public charities, and remarked that Christians suffered in this by comparison.[43]

The third section of the work, on "the Turkish militia", was in the author's eyes the most important and demonstrable of his topics, since the "the Ottoman Constitutions, Laws, Customs and Manners of Living are wholly agreeable to the warlike discipline of a camp." The "great nerve or sinew of the Turkish Empire was its immense force of "Zaims and Timariots", or "Spahees", i.e., landholding cavalrymen. Their number could be computed; it was at least 83,380[44], a number that placed little burden on the imperial treasury. It was the most important factor in Ottoman military power. Rycaut's quantification, however, did not give an objective assessment of Ottoman power, or present military strengths. By the middle of the seventeenth century there had been a sharp falling off in the effectiveness of the Ottoman ruling class. The standards of the previous century were sacrosanct to Ottoman reformers who sought with some success to regain those levels in the present. Decline was particularly advanced in the *timar* system of landholding, local administration, and military service, by which cavalry men held tenures in return for service. Rycaut's sources may have been out of date, or the numbers computed may have represented in fact inferior substitutes for feudal cavalrymen, or men from the private retinues of Ottoman officials. His tables of provinces and soldiers give no hint of the decline of the feudal system and the growth in its place of large privately owned estates (çiftlik) carrying no military obligation, nor do they take account of the spread of tax farming.[45]

Other cavalry units included the salaried "Spahees" and "the more elevated Spahees, called Mutafaraca." They were, however, more of a liability than an asset. They fueled "Combustions in Asia" and were not, by "modern standards" well armed. "Many of them," Rycaut says, "are armed with Bows and Arrows, and with Pistoles and Carbines; but esteem not much of firearms, having an opinion that in the field they make more noise than execution."

Rycaut's assessment of the Janissaries was summed up in his chapter-title: "Whether the Maintenance of an Army of Janissaries according to the original institution be now agreeable to the rules of Politie among the Turks." He thought not. He set their present number at 20,000, but believed their pay and privileges were more suited to a force of 100,000. He linked the disappearance of discipline to the influx of Turks into the Corps. It had become a danger to the ruler, and Rycaut believed that Ahmet Köprülü meant to destroy it.[46]

Rycaut's third section concluded with a variety of topics; descriptions of army encampments between Istanbul and Belgrade, descriptions of Sofia, of Bulgarian peasant girls in traditional costume, and an assessment of Ottoman naval strength. Rycaut found Sofia pleasant enough:

a place so wholly Turkish that there is nothing that appears more antique then the Turks themselves, It is situated in a pleasant plain or broad Valley, between two high mountains, the highest of them wearing a snowy head in the heat of the summer Solstice.

Peasant girls in Bulgaria reminded him of "pictures of the ancient shepherdesses in Arcadia."[47]

The Ottoman encampments were impressively clean. The discipline and sobriety of the soldiers was "a demonstration undeniable of some superior eminent Order in their Army." Still, they had tasted defeat in 1664 on the Raab against the

Habsburgs, and Rycaut was glad "to declare that occasion that put a hook in the nostril of this great Oppressor and diverted him for the present time from further spoil of Christendom."[48] The Ottoman Empire remained a vast land power, but was no longer a sea power. God had reserved the sea for Christians, he solemnly announced. For the unlucky immediate neighbors of the Ottoman Empire "the peril is unrelenting," but as for England, the seas protect her from "the Red and Yoke of this great Oppressor." Between the two realms, there can be only "our Peace and Trade."[49]

In 1667 Rycaut left Istanbul for Izmir, where he was consul for the next decade. He was now a Fellow of the Royal Society, and "a man of letters." He prepared his work on the Greek and Armenian Churches, and a short work, published anonymously, on the Jewish messianic leader Sabbatai Sevi. Rycaut called him a "vile impostor," a Satanic leader of a deluded people. When Ahmet Köprülü offered him the choice of apostasy or execution, he chose the former. The state had won a just triumph over fanaticism.[50]

Another project came to Rycaut from the Royal Society. The Society submitted to him in Izmir a list of 23 questions, "Inquiries for Turkey," embracing botany, geography, zoology, animal husbandry, opiates and poisons, damasco steel and leather-making, other arts and trades worthy of learning, earthquakes, mummies, and Sultan Süleyman's aqueducts at Istanbul.[51] Rycaut responded in November, 1677 in a letter to Henry Oldenbourg, Secretary of the Royal Society and it was by him laid before the Society. He wrote that he had been ill, having suffered from the plague in Istanbul, a naturally unhealthful place made more so by the passage of slaves through the city. He now had time to answer fifteen of the questions. Most interesting among the answers were those on opium, the flow of water from the Black Sea into the Dardanelles, the ways of dressing leather, and the effects of coffee. "Most Turkes dye with a pain in the stomache," he writes, "and many physicians attribute it to their excesse in Coffee . . .

Probably most shocking to his colleagues were his comments on "works of antiquity in these parts."

In most places where I came nothing but confused ruins appearing: antient inscriptions that I have found in Greeke, engraved in stone, being as it were purposely beaten out with hammers . . .

The most memorable of his responses was a description of "Mt. Caucasus":

I have spoken with some who have passed neare Mt. Caucasus, but never over it; but being men who travelled for necessitie, were able to render me a weake acct. of it, as to its position, or temper, more than it is exceeding high, craggy, and horrid, casting a shadow a dayes journey from it.[52]

Rycaut's major work during the stay in Izmir was *The Present State of the Greek and Armenian Churches* (1679). The present state was a sad one: "most mechanicks amongst us [are] more learned and knowing then the Doctors and Clergy of Greece.[53] He preferred the Turkish abhorrence of religious images to the Greeks' ikons and idolatry.[54] The Ottoman authorities were glad to rule through the Greek clergy, and to protect the Church from pogroms. Ahmet Köprülü relied chiefly on Greeks as interpreters and favored the Greek Church in Jerusalem.[55] On the Aegean Islands the Turks had done away with the ruinous taxes of the Venetians, and the Greeks there now "pipe and dance Promiscuously." There was greater religious freedom on the Islands than anywhere else in the Empire.[56] The author's dislike for the Armenian Church, and people, was extreme. The clergy were numerous and idle, and the believers dull and stupid in all things except trade.[57]

Throughout his stay in Turkey, Rycaut collected information for a historical narrative, which began to appear after his return to London in 1679.[58] In it he drew attention to the Ottoman campaign in Crete, which had begun in 1645. In Rycaut's account, the siege of Candia was presented as the most extraordinary siege in history.[59] He mentioned, but did not comment upon, how the English, French and Dutch ships showed "industry and diligence" in supplying the Ottomans with corn. The Venetians evacuated the island in 1669;[60] though fighting had been costly to the victors, they scrupulously observed the terms of the surrender.[61]

Before turning to the flighting in Hungary and Poland Rycaut digressed on the affects of opium. It induced cheerfulness in the heart, and stupefaction in the head. Young Turks prefer wine, but the older men were used to opium. They would

> sit grave and quiet without doing hurt to any man, which is a qualification counted very laudable amongst them and is one of the greatest liberties which they endeavour to acquire in their monasteries.[62]

Finally noteworthy in the book are the hopeful prospects sketched out for the year 1675. The Ottomans had crushed several serious revolts in the previous year; there were royal festivals planned for 1675, and merchants were prosperous and respected. A new customs house opened at Izmir, which Rycaut hoped would make that port the world's greatest emporium in East-West trade. He was glad to note the "happy state of the Ottoman court."[63]

Paul Rycaut was unquestionably the dominant figure in English writing on the Turks in the second half of the century. When Rycaut's second publisher in 1687 appended his work to Knolles', Rycaut reacted angrily: "I cannot but with some Regrett think it a grand disparagement to that Worke, to . . . become an appendix to an old Obsolete author.[64] He made his name with *The Present State of the Ottoman Empire . . .* ; the immense number of editions in several languages has already been noted. Samuel Pepys mentioned it as a study of the "Policy and actions of the Turks, which is, it seems, now much read up," and pronounced it "a very good book."[65] What was its appeal? It lay perhaps in brevity, as Knolles' strength lay in length and weight. *The Present State*, though brief, was formidable. Rycaut's credentials were excellent. He seemed close to the Palace, at the heart of an Empire righting itself internally and moving again on its frontiers. He told sensational tales, and mixed them with computations that appealed to his mercantile, statistical mind. He alluded to parallels in the recent history of Ottoman Turkey and Stuart England. He quoted from Tacitus in describing the Ottomans' present state, and saw the hand of Machiavelli in Istanbul. His topic was troubling, fascinating and distant, but once again, reassuringly delineated.

6

The Road to Vienna

The last quarter of the seventeenth century was a disastrous period in Ottoman history, marked by terrible military defeats and the loss of important imperial lands, including Hungary, to the Austrian Habsburgs. Yet the quarter began auspiciously, with no hint of impending catastrophe. While Ottoman forces in the Ukraine were concluding a campaign that brought the Ottoman Empire to its largest territorial extent, in the summer of 1675 the Ottoman court was in Edirne, enjoying the great royal festivals of Sultan Mehmet IV. The English Embassy, seeking another favorable modification of the English Capitulations, made the trip from Istanbul to Edirne, to meet there with the Grand Vizir Ahmet Köprülü. After the successful conclusion of negotiations, the English returned to Istanbul.

Ahmet Köprülü died in 1676. His successor, described by the leading modern historian of The Levant Company as the "nightmare vizier"[1] was Kara Mustafa Paşa. He mounted a major Ottoman offensive in Hungary in 1682, but lost his army in the defeat at Vienna in 1683, and his life to imperial executioners at Belgrade shortly thereafter. A long and ruinous war against the Habsburgs had begun; defeats in Hungary and upheavals in Istanbul led to the deposition of Mehmet IV in 1687. The war continued until 1699, when at the Treaty of Karlowitz the Ottomans relinquished Hungary, Transylvania, Dalmatia, the Morea, Podolia, and the Ukraine. These events ended, with stunning speed, the threat of Ottoman domination over Europe. The world of Islam had been defeated in the world of war. Old truths seemed to dissolve in the terrible years between 1683 and 1699.

In those dark years of the Ottoman Empire no single English writer emerged with the impact of Knolles or the early Rycaut to chart the course of Empire or assess its changing character. There were Rycaut's own later narrative histories, written from a broad European perspective, and stressing the battles in Hungary. Beyond that, English writing offered the latest news of the fighting, and later, some new approaches to the Ottoman Empire and the Turkish language.

The first of the new writers was a diarist, John Covel, Company Chaplain from 1670 to 1677. His diary was not published until modern times. It contained fascinating descriptions, particularly of Mehmet IV's festivals at Edirne in the Summer of 1675. Covel's approach was much different from that of the previous chaplain, Thomas Smith. Smith had seen only ignorance and barbarism in his surroundings, a condition he traced to Islam.[2] Covel, on the contrary, found his strange ministry endlessly fascinating. "All things being quite so different from our own way of living did very much surprise me with wonder and delight."[3] When he described the journey of the Company officers from Istanbul to Edirne in 1675, his diary has the quality of a traveller's journal. For instance:

> Burgas is a pretty large market town. We passed over a pretty street or two; then came a most stately *chane*, having a fair square court and large fountain in the middest of it, and cloysters roundabout, and then fine apartments able to hold well nigh 1000 travellers with their beasts. . . . Entering into the Khane (for you must pronounce it in the throat) sit many shopkeepers; amongst the rest the finest tobacco-pipe-heads are sold there that are to be found in Turkey.[4]

Approaching Edirne from the East, he says,

> The City begins to appear about 4 or 5 mile of it, indeed it shows gloriously, as all their citys doe at a distance, but within they are very mean and beastly, The Moschs and Minarys (or steeples . . .) are very stately, especially Sultan Selim's. . . .[5]

Once they arrived, they met with Ahmet Köprülü and inquired about the Capitulations. He

> smiled, and said that it was a time of mirth, and great matters were laid aside awhile. . . . The Vizier was always very brief and sparing in his words, whether out of a formall gravity, or the reall Turkish humour of taciturnity, I know not. He look't very pleasantly. . . .[6]

Covel's images of the Ottoman "time of mirth" are the most kaleidoscopic and entertaining to be found in the English literature on the Turks. Covel relished all that he saw, and shared in the good humor of his hosts. The festivities began with a great procession:

> First come by severall companyes of Janizaryes with their Cherbigees or Colonells on foot . . . , then as many more Janizaryes, with the Janizary Aga (a devilish severe figure both in shew and nature and practice). . . . One thing is remarkable, that whereas our swordsmen never go in companys thus but armed . . . , here the devil of sword, gun, or weapon never should you see. . . . Then were carried by 40 Nacules, 20 on a side, which are devices made upon a large pole in frame of a pyramid or cone (rather) of wire, painted paper, and beggars batten (such as we trim hobby horses withall) and flours, and fruit of wax work and printed paper. . . . It was the most gaudy magnificent piece of (Hobbyhorsism) folly. . . .[7]

Then came the Sultan, "his hand big but very rude, *alla Turchesa*; the upper part of his face something resembling Mehemet the first in Knolles. . . .[8] "Dances and sports" and "very excellent fireworks" followed. Some of the dancers he saw

> danc't 4, 5, sometimes 8 in a company. It consists most in wriggling the body (a confounded wanton posture, and speakes as much of Eastern treachery as dumb signs can). . . .[9]

Descriptions of snakehandlers, jugglers, magicians, wrestlers, tricksters, plays, royal coaches, etc. were all in good humor. Once, at the Selimiye mosque, a lusty fellow would needs slide down (a rope from the top of a minaret) with a boy at his back with a drum and stick to beat it: just as they came halfway the rope broke, and down they fell upon a poor Armenian who was standing in the garden amongst others to view the sight. All thre was pretty hurt and bruised, but it pleased God all thre recovered. The G. Sr. paid for their cure, and offered the Armenian a pension, . . . but he, thanking him . . . desired nothing else but that he might have 12 purses of money paid him which a great Basha had owed him. . . The G. Sr. gave orders that it should be done. I have seen him since well enough recovered.[10]

The English were treated as welcome guests:

We found the greatest civility imaginable, and were severall times treated with sherbet of lemmons (once with coffee and sweet meats in a large room): the Aga who carried us in telling us that it would be a shame for us to come to the wedding of the G. Sr.'s daughter and neither eat nor drink.[11]

The festivals ended in June; in July the plague broke out in Edirne. With upwards of 900 deaths daily in the town, the English left town for the countryside.: "We endur'd at the tents and I assure you there is no preservative like a merrie heart and a drame of the bottle".[12] With the award of the new Capitulations in July, the Embassy could return to Istanbul.

Another Company officer whose recollections likewise did not appear until later was Dudley North. He had come to Turkey in 1661 as a Company apprentice, and became Company Treasurer, remaining in that post until 1680. He was said to have been instrumental in the successful renegotiation of the Capitulations, and to have rivalled Rycaut in expertise on the Ottomans. His works were lost, and his knowledge survived only in the recollections his brother had of their conversations, published in 1744. He believed that in spite of a quarter century of relatively moderate rule under the "cupperli" vizirs, the Ottomans were still intent on the conquest of Europe.[13]

In English eyes, the catastrophes that befell the Ottoman Empire after 1676 were prefigured and justified by what observers described as the grasping and vulpine attitude of Kara

Mustafa Paşa towards merchants.[14] His policies in Istanbul foretold his defeat at Vienna and his death in Belgrade. Paul Rycaut's *The History of the Turks Beginning with the Year 1679* cited the death of Ahmet Köprülü and the accession of Kara Mustafa Paşa as a turning point in Ottoman history. Moderation disappeared in a wave of intemperate extortions, injustices and cruelties, the chief victims of which were foreign merchants. Kara Mustafa's demands on them transcended "the bounds of common humanity". Avarice subverted the whole fabric of government, and cast out caution and the ability to make realistic judgments. It was easy for the French to incite the Turks to exploit Protestant discontent in Hungary by attacking there. Rycaut voiced some sympathy for Hungarian Protestant rebels in their struggle against what he called "Romanist" persecution.[15] They faced a difficult choice, between Turkish and German slavery, and although they will be blamed, he thought, for loosing the Turks on Christendom, Rycaut would let his readers judge their case. He thought that natural law, and need for self preservation were on the rebels' side. In the fighting that followed the reckless Ottoman offensive, God had mercifully spared the rebels, taking vengeance instead on the Turks, enemies of all Christendom.[16] Rycaut believed this to be the Ottomans' own interpretation of their defeats from 1683 to 1699: that God had deserted them.[17]

Although the Turkish danger had receded by the early eighteenth century, the last of the wars of Louis XIV of France, the War of the Spanish Succession, still raged in Europe. During the great struggle against "the Sun King" known also as "the Christian Turk",[18] it was harrowing to recall the Turks at Vienna in 1683. Daniel Defoe wrote in 1715 that in 1683 he had written a pamphlet (now lost) on the Turkish attack:

> . . . The Turks were besieging Vienna, and the Whigs in England, generally speaking, were for the Turks' taking it, which I having read the History of the Cruelty and perfidious Dealings of the Turks in their Wars, and how they had rooted out the Name of the Christian Religion in above Threescore and Ten Kingdoms, could by no means agree with . . . and

95

wrote against it. I had rather the Popish House of Austria should ruin the Protestants in Hungary than the Infidel House of Ottoman should ruin both Protestant and Papist, by over-running Germany. . . .[19]

In 1704 he recalled that

In those days we had abundance of People, that had so little sense of Publick Safety, and so much zeal for the Protestant Religion in Hungaria, that they wish'd every day the Turks should take Vienna.[20]

Defoe blamed both the French and the Hungarian rebels for encouraging the Ottoman attack, a mistake for which the rebels paid a severe but just price after the Turks' defeat.[21]

The Ottomans did not accept defeat easily. They fought on grimly after 1683 and recaptured Belgrade in 1690. Neither they nor the Habsburgs would relent in what had become a struggle for Hungary. The war was not one-sided, as the Ottomans fought desperately and at times successfully, at least postponing a final decision and an imposed peace. The fact that England desired an end to the fighting, especially after 1688, was not decisive in of itself. The new King, William III, wanted the Habsburgs to shift their energies from Hungary to Europe, against France. The English cloth trade reached its nadir in 1696[22] and there may have been some worry over Russian expansion in the region of the Black sea, in the face of an Ottoman collapse.[23] Still, there could be no peace in Hungary until after 1697, when the terrible Prince Eugene of Savoy completely destroyed an Ottoman army at the Battle of Zenta. Sultan Mustafa II (1695-1703) barely escaped from the carnage. The new Grand Vizir, Hüseyin Köprülü, was convinced of the necessity of peace, at almost any price:

the price for defeat on the battlefields of Europe was formal recognition of major territorial excisions. Realization for the necessity of these concessions must have been painful for a state whose initial, avowed and expressed justification had been based on the concept of an ever expanding frontier.[24]

Hüseyin Köprülü appealed to England for help in ending the war. He requested that the English Ambassador, Sir William Paget (1697-1702) arrange for negotiations with Austria on the basis of *uti possidetis* (each side retaining its present holdings) as the basis for what became the Treaty of Karlowitz, 1699.

The Treaty was surprisingly favorable to the Turks. They negotiated skillfully, and displayed their knowledge of contemporary English and European affairs. They were aware, for example, of the imminent War of the Spanish Succession. Still, there was no choice but to give up the Morea to Venice. The Turks kept the important heights around Athens. They surrendered Podolia and the Ukraine to Poland, but insisted on the Polish evacuation of Moldavia. The Ottomans gave up Hungary, Transylvania, and Croatia, but insisted that the Habsburgs evacuate and demolish most of the border fortresses left in their possession. Russia fought on alone to capture Azov in 1702, but the Ottomans recaptured it in 1711. In 1715 they recaptured the Morea from Venice and in 1739 regained Belgrade. Nevertheless, after 1683 there were no further Ottoman threats to the whole of Europe. After 1699 they relied to a greater extent on diplomacy and to a lesser extent on force in their dealings with their European adversaries. Institutional changes in the conduct of Ottoman diplomacy date from this period. As the Empire became increasingly defensive in its relationship with Europe, the *reisülküttab*, formerly the chief of the secretaries in the Grand Vizir's chancery, took on the duties of a foreign minister.[25]

By the end of the century, it was France and "the Christian Turk", not the Ottoman Empire, which threatened to dominate Europe.

Alongside these considerations of the high politics of the two Empires, the balance of power in Europe, and the co-existence of religions, other European writings of this period yielded a variety of hastily drawn images of the decadence and defeat of the Ottoman Empire. In 1677 a translation of a fanciful work by Francois Chassepol breathed decadence in its very title alone: *The History of the grand visiers Mahomet and Achmet Caprogli, of the three last Grand Signiors, their Sultana's and chief favourites, with the most secret intrigues of their Seraglio. Besides severall of the particulars sof the wars.* . . . In 1684 readers could find a list of arms, trophies, and riches taken from the Turkish camps around Vienna, in John Peter's *A Relation or Diary of the Siege of Vienna.* In the next year Jean Prechac's *The Seraquier Pasha. An Historical Novel of the Times . . . The True History of Cara Mustafa Pasha* (one of the earliest English uses of the expression "historical novel") treated readers to the violent death of the Grand Vizir. The public also continued to see Turks on the stage. Plays like Gilbert Swinhoe's *The Tragedy of the Unhappy Fair Irene,* gave audiences ornate webs of palace intrigue, star-crossed love, and tragic deaths. Mary Pix' *Ibrahim the Thirteenth Emperour of the Turks: A Tragedy* was typical. Nicholas Rowe's *Tamerlane* (1702) was more political in tone. Tamerlane might have been William III and Bayezit the Thunderbolt perhaps Louis XIV, the first virtuous, the second vice-ridden—a complete change of roles since Marlowe's *Tamburlaine,* in which Bayezit is the pitiful victim. Bayezit is addressed so:

> Why sought'st thou not from they own impious Tribe a wife, like one of these? For such thy race (if humane nature brings forth such) affords. Greece, for chaste virgins famed, and pious matrons, teems not with monsters, like your Turkish wives; whom guardian eunuchs, haggard and deformed, whom walls and bars make honest by constraint.[26]

Letters Writ by a Turkish Spy (1687) is the first example in English of a literary genre later carried to perfection by Montesquieu in his *Persian Letters.* The first of eight volumes was a translation of *L'Espion du Grand Seigneur* (Paris, 1684) by Giovanni Paolo Marana; the other volumes which appeared during the years between 1687 and 1694 are anonymous, and all are spurious. The letters purport to be reports to officials in Istanbul by "Mahmut the Arabian", their secret agent in Europe, who described for them the strange and exotic customs of the Europeans. The result is the kind of criticism of European institutions that became well known during the Enlightenment.[27]

Travel literature tended again to be in translation, from French. In 1677 Jean Baptiste Tavernier provided exotic descriptions of the amusements of potentates in an Oriental despotism. Guillaume Grelot's *A Journey to Constantinople* (1683) was an even stronger intimation of what might today be called "orientalism." Grelot travelled in disguise and claimed to know Turkish; he wrote and sketched well, conveying a sense of travel as a pleasant diversion for gentlemen. Constantinople offered an opportunity to see "the delectable situation of places," the ruins of the ancient past, and "the magnificence and grandeur of the Eastern Emperours.[28] *The Travels of Monsieur de Thévenot into the Levant* appeared in 1687. Thévenot had travelled in 1655, but the picturesque contents spanned the years. He described the beauty of Istanbul and the natural humanity of the Turks, pointing out their robust health, sensible dress, simple diets, and wholesome amusements. Their language was primitive, but grave and pleasant.[29] Thévenot's dislike for Islam was perfunctory, and he went on to say, "It is certain that the Turks are good people and observe very well that command of Nature: not to do to others but what we would have others do to us."[30] But the renegade inhabitants of the palace and harem were another matter. It was the Turks' great misfortune that political power had come into the hands of morally crippled slaves. Because the Sultan never "beats his Brain about Business," he is powerless in the face of his Janissaries.[31]

A work revelling in Ottoman weaknesses was Joanot du Vigneau's *A New Account of the Present Condition of Turkish Affairs, with the Causes of the Decay of the Ottoman Power* (1688). It aimed to

show the Christian World that this great Coloss, which has been hitherto respected as Impregnable, stands on Foundations easily . . . overthrown, as subsisting by such Prejudices and false Descriptions as have been made of its Greatness.[32]

The factors which had in the past made for Ottoman strength—tyranny, slavery, religion, the Köprülü vizirs, misleading Western literature, the crafty ability to attract and profit from foreign merchants -- were now no more. The rulers were lax and immoral, Turks were now found in military and administrative positions, corruption was rampant, and all the while the Ottomans pridefully ignored the outside world. "Cannot Christendom," he asked, "now understand her self in this Subject? If we would express the force and Bravery of a Man we compare him to a Turk, fierce as a Turk. In a word, this name is a mere Phantom to afright children."[33]

Travel literature also offered backward glances at lost worlds. Most remote of all was the world of royal tombs and mosques from the first Ottoman capital, Bursa. Thomas Smith's description of Bursa was almost sentimental in places; the overriding impression made is that of a town of ghosts and memories from the earliest halcyon days of the Ottoman dynasty.[34] Smith's account appeared in an anthology of travel writing in 1693. The next year saw the first English translation of Ogier Busbecq's account of the Ottoman Empire at the summit of its greatness, in the reign of Sultan Süleyman. It was now over a century since the greatest of the Sultans had died. His had been the tenth successful consecutive reign in Ottoman history. Of his successors, two had been killed and three removed from the throne, while the relationship between the Ottoman Empire and Western Europe had changed forever.

The changed nexus of European-Ottoman relations coincided with a new approach to Turkey, through the Turkish language. There were some Latin grammars available in the seventeenth century, including William Seaman's, from 1670. But the study of Turkish in English, a pre-requisite for any deep and accurate knowledge of Turkish history and culture, began with Thomas Vaughan's *A Grammar of the Turkish Language*, published in 1709.[35] Vaughan intended the work for merchants, travellers, and "the public Good." Visitors should avoid close contact with Turks, but should be able to conduct a "civil and humane" conversation:

. . . it's to be remembered that if I know not the meaning of the Voice, I shall be unto him that speaketh a barbarian, and he that speaketh shall be a barbarian unto me. And whoever observes it shall find the treatment he meets with from most people as well abroad as at home (for the World is all of a Piece) answerable to the thoughts they may entertain of him.[36]

Vaughan hoped to introduce reason and the principles of "universall English grammar" into the study of foreign languages. Turkish is best learned by mastering reasonable rules and principles, and then bringing them to bear in conversation. Students should give particular attention to forming nouns from verbs, and to memorizing dialogues and proverbs.

Vaughan's first lesson was on an Ottoman bill of exchange, in Arabic characters. On the following page it was reproduced in Latin characters. There followed a running translation and instantaneous explanations. The lesson concluded with the days of the week and the months of the year. There were 21 lessons in all, each an exposition of a grammatical topic. The lessons are followed by a series of dialogues. These inevitably involve either a merchant and his servant, presumably a native speaker, or a Christian encountering Turks on the street. One learns what to say when getting up in the morning, how to tell a servant to go to the bazaar and purchase a particular carpet, how to gather writing materials for a letter to England, and, finally, how to dismiss the servant for the day: "Away, you ass! Begone!" (Hai eshec, hai!) Other dialogues deal with the language of buying and selling, news of English ships in the harbor, their cargo, news from home, and a collection of fables and proverbs.

Vaughan made a bold attempt. A few essential elements of Turkish are there. The spelling is extremely hazardous, but most of the sentences are at least recognizable, provided the reader knows Turkish already. The book offered the advantages of most "teach yourself" books, i/e., a collection of useful phrases, with some grammar. Explanations, if not incomprehensible, are generally weak. A perfect mastery of the book and the vocabulary might well leave the reader unable to converse with anyone. It was the first of its kind.

101

Another new perspective on the Ottoman Empire was perhaps less than half serious. Aaron Hill's *The Full and Just Account of the Present State of the Ottoman Empire* (1710) bears little resemblance to any prior book, let alone its namesake. Hill was a relation of the Ambassador, William Paget, and travelled in the East with a tutor. He declared that he faced many obstacles in reaching a good understanding of the Ottomans. He rushed through some perfunctory condemnations of a state "whose Black Foundation fix's its greatness on the Bloody Overthrow of Injured Princes and the Undistinguished Slaughter of Invaded Nations."[37] Fortunately, however, there was no *inherent* evil: ". . . extremes are to be rejected and a modest medium chosen . . . the same variety of Humour and Morality now reigns in Turkey that is found in Christendom . . . the numerous Mahometans are like ourselves divided into Good and Bad."[38] With his live-and-let-live attitude he liked the gardens, mosques, and palaces of Edirne and Istanbul. Topkapi impressed him as a fitting residence for a glorious but decadent tyrant. He claimed to have toured the *harem*, where he found unparalleled luxuries. By the end of his book he has come around to off-color stories of the escapades and predicaments of Europeans in Istanbul. Some of his favorite stories were: "A merry story of an English Cook who Caught some Turkish Ladies Naked in a Bagnio" (bath), and "A Sudden Conquest of a Lady's Heart."

No literary colossus emerged from this period to take its place beside the earlier works. Part of the reason for this is that the subject matter had changed. The Ottoman Empire, still immense, durable, and dangerous along its new frontiers, was no longer a "mightie Feare". Contemporary writers were searching for new approaches to the Ottoman Empire, itself in the process of adjusting to new realities. Yet for both English writers and Ottoman statesman, the influence of the past would prove to be considerable.

Conclusion

"In terms of the history of Europe, the Ottoman Empire is at once intimate and alien."[1] In the sixteenth and seventeenth centuries, European observers wrote on the Ottomans in familiar and definitive terms. Their images were often vivid, and endured until modern times. Yet they failed to reflect Ottoman realities and instead popularized commonplaces, e.g., ". . . Wheresoever The Grand Siegniour's horse setteth his foote, there the grasse will grow no more."[2] The Ottomans remained alien after all.

Through most of the sixteenth century, English readers interested in the Ottomans read translations of continental authors. By the seventeenth century there was an English presence in the Ottoman Empire, and a literary edifice was in place. Commerce and curiosity sustained English writing on the Turks. English writers believed that they stood above the world of war and within the world of Islam, that they had successfully narrated Ottoman history and explained the workings of the Ottoman state. Yet much that was characteristic of Ottoman history and life lay beyond their powers of explanation. The Ottoman transition from a frontier march to a classical Islamic state, their methods of conquest and administration, the importance of Islamic brotherhoods and orders, the importance of local religious leaders within the Ottoman *millet* system, the conquest of Arab lands, Ottoman culture, and the causes of the Ottoman decline were all difficult for foreign observers to grasp and explain. Depictions of the Ottoman slave system were particularly misleading. It was convenient and satisfying to attribute Ottoman strength to the abilities of Christian-born slaves in high positions in the ruling class, and conversely to explain Ottoman decline by the infiltration of born Muslims into those positions. Metin Kunt's important work, *Servants of the Sultan*, suggests some reasons for the misunderstanding. There were linguistic difficulties and ambiguities and observers tended to focus almost exclusively on Grand Vizirs, the Palace, and the Janissaries, where slaves of the Porte—*kapikullari*—were much in evidence. Such accounts were sometimes anachronistic, or misleading in their emphasis on one means of entry into the ruling class, the *devşirme*, to the exclusion of all others.[3]

Beyond the narration of Ottoman history and the nature of the Ottoman state lay the mainspring of both—the world of Ottoman statecraft, a world whose very existence was never admitted, let alone entered, by foreign observers. How, and for what reasons did the Ottomans determine policy and strategy? How did they judge their choices to be the right ones for the world as they conceived it to be? Observers took the motivating factors for granted. These lay in the Turks' Scythian origins, or in the compulsions of Islam, or in simple avarice, vengeance, or bloodthirstiness. But for particular cases, large and small, such as the rationale of Ottoman policy towards the English, there was silence. English writers believed that the Ottoman Empire and English commerce were right for each other, and that they had found the same savior in the Köprülü grand vizirs. The death of Ahmet Köprülü unfortunately undammed the old insatiable avarice. By the end of the century an initial Eastern question is in sight: how to cope, profitably, with a power whose nature defies reasonable and moderate rule? With such a limited grasp or even sense for the reality of Ottoman policy-making, writers hardly sensed the existence, beyond the world of war and within the world of Islam, of the world of Ottoman statecraft.

How did things look from within that world?

One answer may lie in the career of the Ottoman historian Mustafa Naima (1665-1715). His writing was important in the Ottoman reform literature of the century; like the English observers, he pointed out signs of corruption and weakness. He wrote at length on the qualities of good leadership and the need for a strong ruler. But for Naima

> Muslim history is the entire frame of reference . . . Islam will inevitably triumph . . . The Ottoman system needs much reworking and restoration, but it is good and uniquely good and it is destined to endure.[4]

Naima played an important role in Ottoman statecraft at the end of the seventeenth century, defending in the ruling class the decision of the Grand Vizir Hüseyin Köprülü (1697-1702) to end the "Fourteen Years War" with the Habsburgs. The attack on Vienna was perhaps misguided; certainly the sudden execution of Kara Mustafa Paşa at Belgrade was a mistake. It opened the gates to one disaster after another. Now, after the Battle of Zenta in 1697, Hüseyin Köprülü could stabilize the frontiers, and reinvigorate the state, if military goals were reduced to a level proportionate with the means at hand. The Ottoman state and lands need to be reordered for the struggle to be renewed. Thus, the Grand Vizir's decision to accept the loss of imperial territories in the Treaty of Karlowitz in 1699 was a wise one, worthy of support.[5]

Naima wrote from within the world of Ottoman statecraft and culture. His world bore little resemblance to Western images of compulsive aggression, vulpine greed, religious hostility, and even of Italianate craftiness, "politick and refined." Of all writers it seems that only William Shakespeare perceived or assumed the existence of Ottoman statecraft. It is worthwhile to recall the Venetian senator Brabantio's warning in "Othello":

> We must not think the Turk so unskillful
> To leave the latest which concerns him first
> Neglecting an attempt of ease and gain
> To wake and wage a danger profitless.

Ottoman statecraft, like any other, drew on an accumulated body of knowledge and experience, made judgments from military and financial considerations, and weighed ends and means, possibilities and limitations. Unlike any other, it assumed the superiority of Islamic and Ottoman traditions. Within that framework, "Naima's recommendations were simple, and they worked." Between 1736 and 1739 the Ottomans recaptured Niş and Belgrade, restoring the frontier with the Habsburgs. In 1739, "when peace negotiations with the Austrians were stalled, the Ottoman commander threatened that the road to Vienna was open, and his troops knew the way."[6]

With the return of stability to the Ottoman frontiers, Ottoman culture entered a vigorous new phase known as "the Tulip Period," characterized by an intellectual awakening and marked by a fascination with Western styles. There was an increase in the number of Ottoman emissaries sent abroad and in their reports on what was going on in the West.[7] For the first time the printing press was there to produce works in Ottoman Turkish. Within the Ottoman world, there could be both renewal and change, continuity and innovation. The seeds of this had not been seen by Western visitors, who had been concerned with Turkish belligerency, tyranny, commerce, religion, and exotic doings in the *harem*.

In the end, then, why were the images and depictions by outsiders so numerous and durable? Why the fascination? For one thing, the Turks were truly dangerous to Europe, intimate and alien at the same time, at a greater or lesser distance. For another, they were strange to Europeans, even as they dominated a world familiar to Europe from Biblical and classical times. Last, the images met a need. Curiosity was boundless:

> What newes? Or here you any tidinges
> Of the pope, of the Emperour, or of kinges
> Of Martyn Luther, or of the great Turke,
> Of this and that, and how the world doth worke?[8]

Curiosity had its own reward—a sense of confidence that grew from the belief that these perspectives on danger and difference were the right ones, that a difficult subject had been mastered. Confidence seemed a fitting reward.

Notes

For full bibliographical details on works cited, see the Bibliographies which follow.

Introduction

[1] L. V. Thomas and Norman Itzkowitz, *A Study of Naima* (1972) 146; see also Ezel Kural Shaw and C. J. Heywood, *English and Continental Views of the Ottoman Empire, 1500-1800*, (1972) *passim*.
[2] Barnette Miller, *Beyond the Sublime Porte. The Grand Seraglio of Stamboul* (1931), 7-11, 48; see also N. Penzer, *The Harem* (Philadelphia, n.d.), 18-19.
[3] John Smythe, *Instructions, Observations, and Orders Mylitarie* (1595), 2.
[4] Richard Knolles, *The Generall Historie of the Turkes . . . unto the yeare 1638 . . .*, fifth ed., London, 1638; the quotation is from the author's Introduction, unpaginated.
[5] *Ibid.*, 1059.
[6] *Ibid.*, 132.
[7] *The Diary of John Evelyn* (New York, 1879) Vol. III, 438.

Chapter 1

[1] Halil Inalcik, *The Ottoman Empire. The Classical Age, 1300-1600* (1973), 11. See also Donald E. Pitcher, *A Historical Geography of the Ottoman Empire* (1972), 46, 63.
[2] Giovanni Botero, *Relations of the most famous kingdomes and commonweales of the world . . .* (London, 1630) 508. The captured Sultan is said to have died in a cage, in which he was transported on display from town to town. There were stories that he was also used as a mounting block, and that he died after beating his head against the bars of the cage.
[3] Andrew Hess, "The Ottoman Conquest of Egypt (1517) and the Beginning of the Sixteenth Century World War," *International Journal of Middle Eastern Studies*, IV (1973), 55-96.
[4] For information on the *pax turcica* see Fernand Braudel, *The Mediterranean and the Mediterranean World in the Age of Philip II* (1973), Vol. II; Halil Inalcik, "Ottoman Methods of Conquest," *Studia Islamica*, Fas. II *(1954), 103-129;* C. M. Kortepeter, *Ottoman Imperialism During the Reformation* (1971) Ch. 1; S. J. Shaw, *History of the Ottoman Empire and Modern Turkey*, Vol. 1: *Empire of the Gazis. . . .* (1976), 50-51;

Peter Sugar, *Southeastern Europe under Ottoman Rule, 1351-1804* (1977), 33, 44, 96, 109; T. Stoianovich, "The Conquering Balkan Orthodox Merchant," *Journal of Economic History,* XX (1960) at p. 241.

For Ottoman institutions, see especially Mustafa Akdağ, "Osmanli Imparatorluğu Yukseliş Devrinde Esas Düzen," *Tarih Araştirmalari Dergisi,* VI (1965), 139-166; also Halil Inalcik, *op. cit;* Metin I. Kunt, *The Sultan's Servants* . . . . 1983); and S. J. Shaw, *op. cit.,* ch. v.

On the role of war in the Ottoman system, see "War in the Ottoman System" by D. Walsh, in Bernard Lewis and P. M. Holt (eds.) *Historians of the Middle East* (1962), esp. pp. 263-4. For Elizabethan attitudes to warfare generally, see P. A. Jorgensen, "Theoretical Views of War in Elizabethan England," *Journal of The History of Ideas,* XIII (1952), 469-81; and C. R. Waggoner, "An Elizabethan Attitude toward Peace and War," *Philological Quarterly,* XXXIII (1954), 20-33; also Richard Knolles, *op. cit.,* 1007.

⁵ See most particularly Andrew C. Hess, "The Battle of Lepanto and its Place in Mediterranean History," *Past and Present,* LVII (1972), pp. 53-74. See also Halil Inalcik, "Lepanto in the Ottoman Documents," in *The Ottoman Empire . . . Collected Studies* (1978), Ch. ix; Braudel, 1088. For Elizabethan masques "of a distinctly Levantine cast" held in the aftermath of the battle, see S. C. Chew, *The Crescent and the Rose . . .* (1937), 125.

⁶ Halil Inalcik, *The Ottoman Empire. The Classical Age,* 41.

⁷ Cited in Terence Spencer, "Turks and Trojans in the Renaissance", *Modern Language Review* XLVII, 1952, 330.

⁸ Andrew Hess, *The Forgotten Frontier* (1978) 85-86. See also John B. Wolf, *The Barbary Coast* (1979), 50-54.

⁹ C. M. Kortepeter, *Ottoman Imperialism During the Reformation* . . . (1972), 92, 235-236. See also Shaw, *op. cit.,* 189.

¹⁰ James C. Davis, ed., *Pursuit of Power, Venetian Ambassadors' Reports on Turkey, France, and Spain in the Age of Phillip II.,* 1560-1600 (New York: Harper & Row, 1970), 125-172 esp. 164.

¹¹ Braudel, *op. cit.,* 254. Sir Paul Rycaut made the same point in the seventeenth century. Se his *The History of the Turks Beginning With the Year 1679.* London. R. Clabell, MDCC. Preface.

¹² Lewis Thomas, *op. cit.,* 14. See also Ömer L. Barkan, "The Price Revolution in the Sixteenth Century . . ." *International Journal of Middle Eastern Studies,* VI (1975), 3-28; Suraiya Faroqhi, *Towns and Townsmen of Ottoman Anatolia* (1948); Inalcik, *The Ottoman Empire. The Classical Age* . . . 41-52; and Shaw, 185-186.

¹³ S. A. Skilliter, *William Harborne and the Trade with Turkey.* . . . , (1977), 50-51, 89-91.

¹⁴ Norman Itzkowitz and Max Mote, *Mubadele, An Ottoman-Russian Exchange of Ambassadors* (1970), 1-4; also Bernard Lewis, *The Muslim Discovery of Europe* (1982), 111-112 and J. C. Hurewitz, "Ottoman Diplomacy and the European States System," *Middle East Journal,* XV (1961), 147.

¹⁵ F. L. Baumer, "England, the Turk, and the Common Corps of Christendom," *American Historical Review,* October, 1944, 30. See also Paul Coles, *The Ottoman Impact on Europe* (1968), 148. Also R. B. Mowat, *A History of European Diplomacy* . . . (1928), 82-83. See Garrett Mattingly's *Renaissance Diplomacy,* Ch. XVII, on the use of moralistic language in treaties, especially concerning the Turks.

¹⁶ S. C. Chew, 55. According to R. S. Schwoebel (*The Shadow of the Crescent.* . . .

[1967], p. 113) most of the information in Venetian hands "never filtered beyond the lagoons, and little affected western views of the Turks outside Venice." Also see Franz Babinger, "Die Aufzeichnung des Genuesen Iacopo de Promontorio de Campis über den Osmanenstaat um 1475," *Sitzungsberichte, Bayerische Akademie der Wissenschaften, Phil.-hist. Klasse*, 1956, VIII. Heft, p. 7.

17 H. Inalcik, *The Ottoman Empire. The Classical Age*, 36-37.

18 J. C. Davis, *op. cit.*, 130-131.

19 V. J. Parry, "Materials of War in the Ottoman Empire" in M. A. Cook, ed., *Studies in the Economic History of the Middle East* (1970), 227.

20 Halil Inalcik, "The Ottoman Economic Mind and Aspects of the Ottoman Economy" in *The Ottoman Empire . . . Collected Studies*, ch. x, 207-18. See also other papers by Inalcik in this collection: Ch. xii, "Capital Formation in the Ottoman Empire" and Ch. vi, "The Ottoman State and its Place in World History," 51-58.

21 Inalcik, *The Ottoman Empire. The Classical Age*, pp. 137-38; Shaw, 163-164; N. Sousa, *The Capitulary Regime of Turkey* (1933); Paul Wittek, "The Turkish Documents in 'Hakluyt's Voyages'," *Bulletin of the Institute of Historical Research* XIX (1942), 136 n. and, G. Mattingly, *Renaissance Diplomacy*, Ch. XVIII, "French Diplomacy and the Breaking up of Christendom," [esp. 154-155.]

22 *The Turkish Letters of Ogier Ghiselin de Busbecq* (1633; reprint 1968), 34-35.

23 Knolles, 1388.

Chapter 2

1 D. J. Sahas, *John of Demascus on Islam. . . .* (1972), 96.

2 R. I. Burns, "Christian-Islamic Confrontation in the West: the Thirteenth-Century Dream of Conversion," *American Historical Review*, LXXVIII (1971) at 35.

3 N. K. Daniel, *Islam and the West. . . .* (1960), 22 *et passim*. See also C. M. Jones, "The Conventional Saracens of the Songs of Geste," *Speculum*, XVII (1942), at 203; D. Metlitzki, *The Matter of Araby in Medieval England* (1977), *passim*; D. C. Munro, "Western Attitudes Towards Islam in the Time of the Crusades," *Speculum*, VI (1931), 330-338.

4 Jones, 204, 221, 227; Metlitzki, 200.

5 Daniel Defoe, *An Appeal to Honour and Justice* (1715), 51. See also *Defoe's Review* (reprint 1938), Vol. I, no. 56 (September 16, 1704), 237-239.

6 Metlitzki, 222-223.

7 C. Rouillard, *The Turk in French History . . .* (1979), 42-45.

8 Pope Pius II, "A Call for Common Action Against the Turks" (1459), in *The Portable Medieval Reader*, ed. J. B. Ross and M. M. McLaughlin (1972), 320.

9 John D'Amico, *Renaissance Humanism in Papal Rome. . . .* (1983), 216-219.

10 R. Schwoebel, *The Shadow of the Crescent. . . .* (1967), 19.

11 A. Cambini, *Two Commentaries* (1976 reprint), 30-31.

12 K. M. Setton, "Pope Leo X and the Turkish Peril," *Proceedings of the American Philosophical Society*, CXIII (1969), 369-75.

13 Michael J. Heath, "Renaissance Scholars and the Origin of the Turks," *Bibliothèque d'Humanisme et Renaissance*, XLI (1979) 454-471. See also Terence Spencer, "Turks and Trojans in the Renaissance".

14 See Machiavelli, *The Prince*, Chapter iv: "Why the Kingdom of Darius, Occupied

by Alexander, Did not Rebel against the Successors of the Latter after his Death," for Machiavelli's comparison of the French and Turkish "kingdoms."

[15] Nicolo Machiavelli. *The Chief Works and Others* (1965), 14, 21. ·

[16] Erasmus, *Enchiridion* (1963), 128.

[17] Erasmus, *Praise of Folly* (1947), 196. For Erasmus' attitude, see R. P. Adams, *The Better Part of Valor* (1962), 163-164, 171. See also 26 for Vives' criticisms of Henry VIII for failing to recognize the extent of the Turkish danger in 1526, the year of the Battle of Mohacs.

[18] See K. J. Wilson, "More and Holbein: The Imagination of Death," *Sixteenth Century Journal*, VII (1976), 51; and R. J. Schoeck, "Thomas More's 'Dialogue of Comfort' and the Problem of the Real Grand Turk," *English Miscellany*, XX (1969), 29-30, 33.

[19] K. M. Setton, "Lutheranism and the Turkish Peril," *Balkan Studies*, III/1 (1962), 147.

[20] Senol Ozyurt, *Die Türckenlieder and das Türckenbild.* . . . (1977), 21. See also J. W. Bohnstedt, *The Infidel Scourge of God: the Turkish Menace.* . . . (1958), 32.

[21] K. M. Setton, 141-142. See also R. Ebermann, *Die Türckenfurcht.* . . . (1904), *passim;* also R. Schwoebel, "Co-existence, Conversion, and Crusade . . . ," *Studies in the Renaissance*, XII (1965) at p. 173.

[22] G. W. Forell, "Luther and the War Against the Turks," *Church History*, XIV (1945), 258, 264; also Setton, *op. cit.*, 151.

[23] Bohnstedt, 33; Setton, 153-63.

[24] S. C. Chew, 102-103 n.

[25] See Steven Fischer-Galati, *Ottoman Imperialism and German Protestantism 1527-1565* (1969).

[26] Setton, 162.

[27] See Franz Babinger, *Die Geschichtschreiber der Osmanen.* . . . (1927), 73; Michael Heath, 454; J. A. B. Palmer, "The Origin of the Janissaries," *Bulleton of the John Rylands Library*, XXXV (1952-53), 476; and Lewis and Holt, 179. C. von Spiegel published an Ottoman chronicle in German in 1567. Later English writers, such as Richard Knolles, used it as a source. It was probably this chronicle that Hans Löwenclau (Leunclavius) translated into Latin in 1588, under the title *Annales Sultanórum Othmanidárum, a Turcis sua lingua scripti.* That work has disappeared. The same author published a second translation in 1591, the *Historiae Musulmanae Turcorum.* It was based on a second Turkish chronicle, by an anonymous author, together with a section of the chronicle by Neşri Mehmet Efendi; it appeared in German in 1595.

[28] Salmon Schweigger, *Eine neue Reyssbeschreibung* . . . (1613), 111.

[29] *Ibid.*, 115.

[30] *Ibid.*, 136.

[31] *Ibid.*, 195.

[32] C. Rouillard, 37. For the contribution of Guillaume Postel, *De la Republique des Turcs* (Poitiers, 1560) and of Christophe Richier, *De rebus Turcarum* (1540), see M. J. Heath, "Renaissance Scholars and the Origins of the Turks", *Bibliotheque d'Humanisme et Renaissance*, XLI (1969) 453-471.

[33] Nicolas de Nicolay, *The navigations, peregrinations and voyages made into Turkey.* . . (1585) See Paul Coles, *The Ottoman Impact on Europe* (1968) for illustrations

110

from the French editions of 1568, including the formidable Janissary also to be found on the jacket of C. M. Kortepeter, *op.cit.*

³⁴ N. Penzer, 37.

³⁵ Nicolay, 597-601.

³⁶ J. Schiltberger, *The Bondage and Travels of Johann Schiltberger* . . . (1879) Also, Franz Babinger, 9.

³⁷ J. A. B. Palmer, "Fr. Georgia de Hungaria . . . and the Tractatus de moribus Turcorum" *Bulletin of the John Rylands Library* (1951-1952), 54, 60. Also R. Schwoebel, 208.

³⁸ Quoted in Barnette Miller, *Beyond the Sublime Porte, 63;* and in Inalcik, *The Ottoman Empire. The Classic Age, 79 from Trattato de costume et vita di Turchi,* Florence, 1548, 91.

³⁹ *The Four Epistles of A. G. Busbecq* . . . (1694). For other editions, see Bibliography, Section I.

⁴⁰ Shaw and Heywood, 19.

⁴¹ *Turkish Letters of Busbecq* (1927 ed.) 5

⁴² Busbecq, edition of 1694, 16.

⁴³ *Ibid.,* 24.

⁴⁴ *Ibid.,* 50.

⁴⁵ *Ibid.,* 5, 43, 61, 257.

⁴⁶ *Ibid.,* 103, IV, 145.

⁴⁷ *Ibid.,* 59-61.

⁴⁸ *Turkish Letters of Busbecq* (edition of 1968), 62.

⁴⁹ Edition of 1694, III, 371.

⁵⁰ *Ibid.,* IV, 171.

⁵¹ J. C. Davis, 164.

⁵² Kortepeter, 92. Also J. R. Walsh, "Giovanni Tomasso Minadoi's History of the Turco-Persian War. . . .", *International Congress of Orientalists, Proceedings (Trudy)* Moscow, 1960. Walsh describes Minadoi's *Historia della Guerra fra Turchi et Persiani* (1587), translated into English by Abraham Hartwell (1595) and, according to Walsh, 452, plagiarized by Richard Knolles. According to Walsh the book was factually accurate but marred by a strong anti-Ottoman bias.

⁵³ Geuffroy, lvi, lxi, lxvi.

⁵⁴ *Ibid.,* lxxvii.

⁵⁵ *Ibid.,* lxxix.

⁵⁶ Lewis and Holt, 284.

⁵⁷ *A Shorte Treatise upon the Turkes Chronicles, compyled by Paulus Iovius. . . .* (London, 1546), p. cxv.

⁵⁸ *Ibid.,* xcvii.

⁵⁹ *Ibid.,* cxix, cxxvii, cxxxiiii, cxxxvi.

⁶⁰ Berna Moran, *Türklerle ilgili Ingilizce yayinlar bibliografyasi on beşinci yüz-yildan on sekizinci yüzyila kadar* (1964), 18-19. Also S. C. Chew, 200.

⁶¹ Andrea Cambini, *Two Very Notable Commentaries.* . . . (1562)

⁶² Andrea Cambini, *Two Commentaries.* . . . (1976 reprint), "Epistle Dedicatorie."

⁶³ *Ibid.,* 17.

⁶⁴ *Ibid.,* 32.

⁶⁵ *Ibid.,* 56.

⁶⁶ H. Gough, tr. *The Offspring of the House of Ottomano.* . . . (1570), 60. See also Paul

Coles, *op. cit.*, for illustrations from the first edition, showing chained captives and the punishment of fugitives.

[67] *Ibid.*, 70.

[68] *Ibid.*, 70-93.

[69] Frauncis Billerbeg, *Most Rare and Strange Discourses*. . . . . . , (1585), 2-3, 10-12.

[70] *Ibid.*, 17-47. See also Bernard Lewis, *Istanbul and the Civilization of the Ottoman Empire* (1963) for these descriptions.

[71] *The Ottomano of Lazaro Soranzo* (1603), 10-12.

[72] *Ibid.*, 16.

[73] *Ibid.*, 15-23.

[74] *Ibid.*, 98.

[75] *Ibid.*, 56.

Chapter 3

[1] Hamit Dereli, *Kralice Elizabet devrinde Türkler ve Ingilizler* (1951), 18-19; see also Metitzki, 58-89, 120, 160-161, 199, 249.

[2] *Oxford English Dictionary,* Vol. XI, 479-80.

[3] Roger Ascham, *English Works* (1970), 131.

[4] According to Halil Inalcik (*The Ottoman Empire. The Classical Age*, 138) Sultan Süleyman "granted English merchants the right to trade freely in the Ottoman Empire, but they did not at first exploit the privilege." I know of no other mention or confirmation of this point. On the previous page he gives the date of the first grant of Capitulations to France as 1569, rather than the date commonly given, 1536.

[5] C. M. Kortepeter, 71.

[6] Susan Skilliter, "William Harborne, The First English Ambassador 1583-1588," in William Hale and Ali Ihsan Bağiş, *Four Centuries of Turco-British Relations* (1984) p. 13. Also V. J. Parry in M. A. Cook, 124, and Stanford Shaw, 161.

[7] Susan Skilliter, *Ibid.*, p. 114.

[8] A. K. Meram, *Belgelerle Türk-Ingiliz ilişkileri tarihi* (1969), 14; see also S. A. Skilliter, *William Harborne and the trade with Turkey,* (1977) 50-51, 89-91, 116.

[9] A. L. Rowland, *Studies in English Commerce and Exploration in the Reign of Elizabeth I: England and Turkey* (1924), 18. See also A. L. Hornicker, "William Harborne and the Beginning of Anglo-Turkish Diplomatic and Commercial Relations," *Journal of Modern History,* XIV (1942), 301; Lord Kinross, *The Ottoman Centuries* (1977), 325; Skilliter, 175.

For the argument that The Levant Company existed previously, trading under Venetian auspices, and that this charter (1581) is for the Turkey Company to manage part of the business, see Lansing Collins, "Barton's Audience in Istanbul," *History Today,* XXV (1975), 262-70.

[10] See S. A. Skilliter, *William Harborne* . . . 185-186. For "chambletts" ("stuffs made from the hair of the Angora goat") and "gogroms" ("a coars fabric of silk of mohair and wool") see David French, "A sixteenth-Century English Merchant in Ankara," *Anatolian Studies,* XXII (1972), 242-243. See also Ralph Davis in M. A. Cook. 193-206.

[11] Skilliter, 200.

[12] Rowland, 32.

[13] Horniker, 304; also A. K. Kurat, *Türk-Ingiliz Münasebetlerinin Başlanğici ve Gelişmesi* (1953), 52.

[14] Edwin Pears, "The Spanish Armada and the Ottoman Porte", *English Historical Review*, VIII (July, 1893), 439-466, includes much of Barton's correspondence, and attaches great importance to Spanish bribes to Ottoman officials. Also see Lansing Collins, "Barton's Audience in Istanbul", *History Today*, XXV, April, 1975, 263, G. B. Harrison, *The Elizabethan Journals*, Vol. I., 188, I. J. Podea, "A Contribution to the Study of Queen Elizabeth's Eastern Policy 1590-1593", *Melange d'histoire general*, 1936, 423-424, 469-470, and Paul Wittek, The Turkish Documents in 'Hakluyt's Voyages'" *Bulletin of the Institute of Historical Research*, XIX, (1942), 121-123.

[15] Conyers Read, *Mr. Secretary Walsingham* (1926) 226.

[16] Stanford Shaw, 182-183.

[17] V. J. Parry, "Barud," *Encyclopedia of Islam*, 1061-1066.

[18] S. Skilliter, "Three letters from the Ottoman 'Sultana' Safiye to Queen Elizabeth I," in S. M. Stern, ed., *Documents from Islamic Chanceries* (1965), 149.

[19] See "The Diary of Thomas Dallam, 1599-1600" in *Early Travels and Voyages into the Levant*, J. T. Dent, ed. (1893), 69, 73, 140; also Stanley Mayes, *An Organ for the Sultan* (1956) and S. C. Chew, 171.

[20] Richard Hakluyt, comp., *The Principall Navigations, Voyages, and Discoveries of the English Nation* (reprint 1965), 81-82.

[21] *Ibid.*, 205-206.

[22] D. French, 243.

[23] *The Travels of John Sanderson in the Levant* (reprint, 1931).

[24] *Ibid.*, 57.

[25] *Ibid.*, 141. See also Cecil Roth, *The House of Nasi* (1948), 27, for another report of Murat's accession which reached the English Embassy at the time.

[26] *The Travels of John Sanderson*, 62.

[27] *Ibid.*, 80.

[28] *Ibid.*, 70.

[29] *Ibid.*, 78.

[30] *Ibid.*, 191.

[31] Fynes Moryson, *An Itinerary Containing His Ten Yeares Travel. . . .* (1907), 11-17.

[32] Stanford Shaw, 164-165.

[33] Halil Inalcik, "Süleyman the Lawgiver and Ottoman Law" in *The Ottoman Empire . . . Collected Studies*, 105-138.

[34] Moryson, 69.

[35] *Ibid.*, 15, 38.

[36] Inalcik, "Süleyman the Lawgiver" *op. cit.*, 112; and "Ottoman Methods of Conquest," *Studia Islamica*, Fas. II (1954), 103-129.

[37] Moryson, 37, 51.

[38] *Ibid.*, 50-57.

[39] *Ibid.*, 42-47.

[40] *Ibid.*, 70.

[41] *Ibid.*, 69, 122, 131.

[42] A. C. Wood, *A History of the Levant Company* (1935), 60; Michael Strachan, *The Life and Adventures of Thomas Coryate* (1961), 161.

[43] Edward Arber, ed., *An English Garner.* Vol. I, *Voyages and Travels* (1903), 219. E. S. Bates, *Touring in 1600* (1911), 186. The whole topic of piracy and reaction to it is

treated in S. C. Chew, ch. viii, "The Throne of Piracy." Also **Ralph Davis**, "England and the Mediterranean, 1576-1670," in F. J. Fisher, ed., *Essays in the Economic and Social History of Tudor and Stuart England*, (1961), 129; **Berna Moran**, 72; Edward Webbe, *The Rare and Most Wonderful Things which Ed. Webbe . . . hath Seen and Passed. . . .* (1590). For the salient features of the imagery of Algerian pirates, see Wolf, *The Barbary Coast* (1979), 91-111.

    44 Irving Ribner, *The English History Play* (1957), 65.

    45 Cecil Roth, 163-166.

    46 *Ibid.*, 247.

    47 Berna Moran, 150-152.

    48 *The Life of Henry V*, Act V, Scene 2, lines 198-211.

    49 *The Tragedy of Othello*, Act I, Scene 3, lines 20-40.

    50 F. S. Fussner, *The Historical Revolution* (1962), 59; Ribner, 15-26.

    51 Samuel Johnson, *The Rambler* no. 122, May 15, 1751.

    52 On the relationship between Islam and war, see Francis Bacon, "Of the True Greatnesse of Kingdoms and Estates," *Essays*, no. 29 (Classics Club ed., 1942, 127-128):" . . . the Turk hath at hand for cause of war the propagation of his law or sect." Knolles' treatment of individual rulers is prefaced by "The Author's Induction to the Christian reader, unto the Historie following" and is followed by "A briefe Discourse on the greatnesse of the Turkish Empire" after p. 1501 in the edition of 1638. The treatment of Ottoman rulers themselves may have reminded readers of *A Mirrour for Magistrates* (1559; edition of 1960), a well known compilation of short tragedies whose form derived from *De casibus* of Bocaccio. The tragedies are recited by the ghosts of notable but flawed historical figures, whose lives contained forewarnings of inevitable punishments for their misdeeds. See Lily B. Campbell, *Mirror for Magistrates*, New York: Barnes & Noble, 1960. Knolles numbered the Ottoman rulers sequentially, in chapter-titles, reflecting perhaps the influence of numerologically based predictions of the downfall of the Ottoman Empire current during the Renaissance and Reformation; these are discussed by M. J. Heath, 469. See also C. S. Lewis, *English Literature in the Sixteenth Century* (1954), 246.

    53 *The Generall Historie of the Turkes. . . . . .* (1638), 129-135.

    54 *Ibid.*, 171-172.

    55 *Ibid.*, 1390.

    56 *Ibid.*, 200.

    57 *Ibid.*, 333.

    58 *Ibid.*, 349.

    59 *Ibid.*, 350.

    60 *Ibid.*, 353. Knolles was the principal source used by Samuel Johnson in writing *Irene, A Tragedy* (1749).

    61 Knolles, 361.

    62 *Ibid.*, 469.

    63 *Ibid.*, 436.

    64 *Ibid.*, 884-885. Cervantes fought at Lepanto. For his reaction to the deliverance of the galley slaves, see *Don Quixote*, Part I, ch. xxx. See also Jack Beeching, *The Galleys at Lepanto* (1982) 124. According to John Aubrey (*Brief Lives* [1957 ed.]) under Knolles, Knolles' description of the battle moved Lord Burleigh to send for Knolles, who told Burleigh that his chief source of information was a young man who had come to Knolles, "hearing what he was about, and desired that he might write that, having been in that

Action." Lord Burleigh sought to find the man and traced him to Newgate, only to learn that he had been hanged two weeks earlier.

For a different rendering of the quotation re Cyprus, see Garrett Mattingly, *The Armada* (1959), 108.

65 Knolles, 903, 919, 1007.
66 *Ibid.*, 1151.
67 *Ibid.*, 1199.
68 The first figure is given on the fifth page of Knolles' "A Briefe Discourse. . . ."; the second appears on p. 1391 of the edition of 1638 in the section by one of Knolles' continuators, Thomas Nabbes, "A Continuation of the Turkish Historie. . . ."
69 Jean Bodin, *Colloquium of the Seven about Secrets of the Sublime* (edition of 1976), 219.
70 Jean Bodin, *The Six Bookes of a Commonweale*, translated by Richard Knolles (1606), Vol. I, 44.
71 *Ibid.*, II, 85.
72 *Ibid.*, III, 258, and VI, 777.
73 *Ibid.*, IV, 537.
74 *Ibid.*, V, 530.
75 Knolles, *The Generall Historie. . . .*, page 28 of Thomas Nabbes' Continuation in the fifth edition of 1738.
76 Knolles, *The Generall Historie. . . .*, 1055.
77 Knolles, *The Turkish History* (1701), p. 852.

Chapter 4

1 D. H. Willson, *King James VI and I* (1956), 65-66.
2 S. C. Chew, 176.
3 See Braudel, 791; Dereli, *op. cit.*, p. 74; *The Travels of John Sanderson* (1931); Andrew Hess, *The Forgotten Frontier* (1978), 108-109; Hess, "The Moriscos: An Ottoman Fifth Column . . .", *American Historical Review*, LXXIV (1968), 1-25. Also Kurat, 162-64, and H. C. Lea, *The Moriscoes in Spain* (1901), 287.
4 For the topic of Ottoman internal difficulties in the first half of the seventeenth century, see Stanford Shaw, 170-173, 187-190; Braudel, 69, 543-544; Peter Sugar, 10; L. V. Thomas and Norman Itzkowitz, *A Study of Naima* (1972), 14; W. L. Wright, *Ottoman Statecraft* (1935), G. W. Zinkeisen, *Geschichte des Osmanisches Reiches* (1840-63), Vol. III, 247-260.
5 Orhan Burian, *Babaali Nezdinde Üçüncü Ingliz Elcisi Lello 'nun Muhtirasi* (1962), 67.
6 Thomas Roe, *The Negotiations of Sir Thomas Roe. . . .* (1740), 1-3. For Roe and the diplomatic situation generally, see Michael J. Brown, *Itinerant Ambassador: The Life of Sir Thomas Roe (1970)*. See also Joseph von Hammer-Purgstall, *Geschichte des osmanischen Reiches* (1932), Vol. IV, 533-534; Zinkeisen, Vol. III, pp. 654, 845-6.
7 See D. W. Davies, *Elizabethans Errant. The Strange Fortunes of Sir Thomas Sherley and His Three Sons* (1967); also S. C. Chew, 172; Moran, 152.
8 John Smith, *The True Travels, Adventures, and Observations of Captain John Smith. . . .* (1630), 23, 31.
9 Samuel Purchas, *Hakluytes Posthumus, or Purchas his Pilgrimes* (edition of 1905);

Douglas Bush, *English Literature in the Earlier Seventeenth CEntury* (1962), 119; L. B. Wright and C. A. Lamar, eds., *Life and Letters in Tudor and Stuart England* (1962), 119.

[10] Purchas, 42-44.

[11] *Ibid.*, Vol. VIII, 301-320.

[12] *Ibid.*, Vol. VIII, 254-255. For Biddulph, see his *The Travels of certaine Englishmen into Africa*. . . . (1609) and *The Travels of Four Englishmen and a Preacher* (1617).

[13] Purchas, Vol. VIII, 260. The first European visitor to the Ottoman Empire to describe coffee may have been Leonhard Rauwolf, whose description appeared, in German, in 1582. See K. H. Dannenfeldt, *Leonhard Rauwolf* (1968).

[14] Purchas, 264.

[15] *Ibid.*, 278.

[16] *Ibid.*, VIII, 41, 134.

[17] *Ibid.*, 99.

[18] *Ibid.*, 155.

[19] *Ibid.*, 151.

[20] *Ibid.*, 108.

[21] *Ibid.*, 110, 118.

[22] *Ibid.*, 123-124.

[23] *Ibid.*, 121.

[24] *Ibid.*, 128, 127-129.

[25] *Ibid.*, 156-157.

[26] William Lithgow, *The Rare Adventures of William Lithgow* (1632), 36.

[27] See Michael Strachan, *The Life and Adventures of Thomas Coryate* (1961), 294.

[28] Purchas, Vol. X, pp. 416-419.

[29] *Ibid.*, 421.

[30] *The Travels of Peter Mundy*. . . . (ed. of 1907), 21.

[31] *Ibid.*, 55-59.

[32] See Harold Bowen, *British Contributions to Turkish Studies* (1945), 21; S. C. Chew, 94; Bernard Lewis, *Istanbul and the Civilization of the Ottoman Empire*, 180; Berna Moran, 78; and N. Penzer, 35. Penzer cites Ottaviano Bon, *A Description of the Grand Signor's Seraglio, or the Turkish Emperours Court* (1650).

[33] Purchas, Vol. IX, p. 327; Shaw, *op. cit.*, p. 117.

[34] Purchas, 334, 338-347.

[35] *Ibid.*, 338, 353-354.

[36] *Ibid.*, 360.

[37] *Ibid.*, 350.

[38] C. Rouillard, 253. Rouillard cites *Inventaire de l'histoire générale des Turcs* (1617) and *Histoire generale de la Religion des Turcs* (1625).

[39] Michel Baudier, *The History of the Imperiale Estate of the Grand Seigneurs*. . . . (1633), 127-156.

[40] Peter Mundy, *op. cit.*, 184. It had been a commonplace that when the Turks took Constantinople they found there "three hundred million" in gold. See G. B. Harrison, *Elizabethan Journals*, Vol. II, 273.

[41] Giovanni Botero, *Relations of the Most Famous Kingdomes and Common Weales thorowout the world*. . . . (1630), 512.

[42] *Ibid.*, 514-517.

[43] *Ibid.*, 521. William Harborne's figure exactly.

[44] *Ibid.*, 523.

⁴⁵ Thomas Nabbes, "A Continuation of the Turkish History" in Knolles (1638), 1391.

⁴⁶ Sir Thomas Roe, 126.

⁴⁷ *Ibid.*, 45-52.

⁴⁸ *Ibid.*, 153.

⁴⁹ *Ibid.*, 178.

⁵⁰ *Ibid.*, 223.

⁵¹ *Ibid.*, 258.

⁵² Henry Marsh, *A New Survey of the Turkish Empire.* . . . (1633), 82-83, 111.

⁵³ For Blount's life, see Aubrey, *Brief Lives* (1957), 25-27. The poet Henry King saluted Blount's work: "The solid depths of your rare history . . . looks above our gadders' trivial reach. The Commonplace of Travellers who teach but Table Talk and seldomly aspire Beyond the Countreys Diet or Attire." For Blount's works, see Samuel Chews, 24-5, and Berna Moran, 69.

⁵⁴ Sir Henry Blount, *A Voyage into the Levant* (1636), 1-2.

⁵⁵ *Ibid.*, 15.

⁵⁶ *Ibid.*, 22.

⁵⁷ *Ibid.*, 75.

⁵⁸ *Ibid.*, 155.

⁵⁹ *Ibid.*, 61.

⁶⁰ *Ibid.*, 67.

⁶¹ *Ibid.*, 78-89.

⁶² *Ibid.*, 89-95.

⁶³ *Ibid.*, 97-99. See Itzkowitz, *Ottoman Empire and Islamic Tradition*, 87-89 for a good discussion of Ottoman ideas on social and political stability.

⁶⁴ Blount, 126.

Chapter 5

¹ Sir Paul Rycaut, *The History of the Turkish Empire From the Year 1629 to the Year 1677. Containing the Reigns of the last Emperours, viz. Sultan Morat or Amurad IV, Sultan Ibrahim and Sultan Mahomet IV* . . . London, Thomas Basset, 1687, 77. This is the continuation, by Rycaut, of Knolles' *General Historie* in the edition of 1687. (*The Turkish History with Sir Paul Rycaut's Continuation.* Sixth Edition. London: Thomas Basset, 1687.

² Dorothy M. Vaughan, *Europe and the Turk. A Pattern of Alliances.* (1954) 245; Also, C. Rouillard, 417.

³ See Berna Moran, p. 45, for the citation.

⁴ Paul Rycaut, *The History of the Turkish Empire From the Year 1623* . . . In the section "To the Reader" Rycaut gave "The Memoirs of Sir Paul Rycaut . . ." as the title for his work on the years 1660-1678. See p. 328.

⁵ Francis Osborne, *Political Reflections on the Government of the Turks* (1656) 289-295. See Berna Moran, 77, for other editions.

⁶ Osborne, 322.

⁷ Paul Rycaut, "The Memoirs of Sir Paul Rycaut Containing the History of the Turks From the Year 1660 to the Year 1678 With the Most Remarkable Passages Relating to the English Trade . . ." in *The History of the Turks From the Year 1623* . . . "The History of Sultan Mahomet IV . . ." 166.

117

8 For the Köprülü vizirs see *Türk Islam Ansiklopedisi* (the Turkish Enclyclopedia of Islam) 892-896. Also J. von Hammer-Purgstall, Vol. VI; Itzkowitz, *Ottoman Empire and Islamic Tradition*, 79-81; Stanford Shaw, 207-222; Lewis Thomas, *op.cit. passim;* G. W. Zinkeisen, Vol. VI.

9 Paul Cernovodeanu, "The General Condition of English Trade. . . ." *Revue des études sud-est européens*, V (1967), 3-4. Also see Ralph Davis in M. A. Cook, 194-201; Berna Moran 88. A. C. Temple in his edition of *The Travels of Peter Mundy* (1907) cites a description by John Chardin of the trade in Izmir in 1672. See also A. C. Wood, *History of the Levant Company* (1935), 105-111. Paul Rycaut published translations of the English Capitulations for 1663 and 1675; see Sonia P. Anderson, "Sir Paul Rycaut, F. R. S.,. . . .", *Proceedings of the Huguenot Society of London*, XXX (1970 for 1969) at p. 479. See also Rycaut, *Present State of the Ottoman Empire* (1668), 217-218.

10 See *The Works of Isaac Barrow*, Vol. III for two Latin discourses on Islam; also P. H. Osmond, *Isaac Barrow, His Life and Times* (1944) p. 66. describes Barrow's poem "De religione turcica" as a harsh attack on Islam. Aubrey *(Brief Lives,* 17-20) gives stories about Barrow's stay in Istanbul.

11 For neo-Hellenism, see David Constantine, *Early Greek Travellers and the Hellenic Ideal;* J. M. Osborn, "Travel Literature and the Rise of neo-Hellenism in England," *Bulletin of the New York Public Library*, LXVII (1963), 279-300. For problems in Jerusalem see G. P. Abbott, *Under the Turk in Constantinople . . .* , 125; J. M. Neale, *A History of the Holy Eastern Church. . . .* 423-429; Steven Runciman, *The Great Church in Captivity*, p. 267; Paul Rycaut, *The Present State of the Greek and Armenian Churches* (1679), material in the author's preface.

12 M. R. Brailsford, *Quaker Women*, 115, 121.

13 Berna Moran, 84.

14 John Burbury, *A Relation of a Journey of the Right Honourable My Lord Henry Howell. . . . .* (1671), 70, 76.

15 *Ibid.*, 83.

16 *Ibid.*, 109-114.

17 *Ibid.*, 176.

18 *The Reign of Sultan Orchan, Second King of the Turks,* translated by William Seaman (1652), the "Epistle Dedicatory" and Preface. For Saddudin Efendi, see F. Babinger, *Die Geschichtsschreiber . . .* , 126; Stanford Shaw, 146. The first translation of the chronicle, *Cronica dell origine e progresse della casa ottomana da Saidino Turco* was published in Vienna in 1649. Other sections, or versions, appeared in Madrid (1651) and England (1683). For Seaman's own work subsequent to *The Reign of Sultan Orchan* see *The Correspondence of Henry Oldenbourg*, II, 213-214; IV, 217.

19 *The Reign of Sultan Orchan*, 3-5, 9, 25.

20 *Ibid.*, 33.

21 *Ibid.*, 105-106.

22 Abbott, 162. Finch went on to speak of the difficulties of doing business with "Faithless Greeks," "False Jews," and English embezzlers turning Turk.

23 Sonia Anderson, 474-475 *et passim.*

24 George Finch, *Report on the Manuscripts of Allan George Finch.* London (1913). Vol. I., 269, 270. For Paul Rycaut's travels throughout the Ottoman Empire see Sonia Anderson's excellent "Paul Rycaut and his Journey from Constantinople to Vienna in 1665-1666," *Rev. Etudes Sud-Est Europ.* XI, 2, P. 251-173. Bucarest, 1973.

25 Paul Rycaut, "The Reign of Sultan Morat or Amurath IV, 23, 48;" "The Reign of

Sultan Mehmet or Mahomet IV", 83, 88. in *The History of the Turkish Empire From the Year 1623. . .*

²⁶ P. H. Osmond, *Isaac Barrow*, 68. Paul Rycaut, "The Reign of Sultan Mehmet . . . " 88.

²⁷ Paul Rycaut, *The Present State of the Ottoman Empire . . .* (1668). The edition of 1666 was dated 1667 but was destroyed in the Great Fire in London in September, 1666. See Sonia Anderson, p. 474. Subsequent references to Rycaut, unless otherwise noted, are to this work, which is available in a 1970 reprint by Arno (now Ayer). See the "Epistle Dedicatorie."

²⁸ Rycaut, "The Epistle to the Reader", and 42. Bobowski is credited with a number of works, including a Turkish-Latin grammar, a Turkish *New Testament*, or Anglican cathecism in Turkish. See Bibliography under Bobovi. For a fuller discussion of Rycaut's friends and sources of information on the Ottomans, especially as delineated in his later works, see Sonia Anderson, "Paul Rycaut and his Journey . . ." 254.

²⁹ Rycaut, "The Epistle to the Reader."

³⁰ *Ibid.*, Ch. IV., "A true relation of the designs managed by the Old Queen . . . and of the death of the said Queen and her complices," 11-24.

³¹ *Ibid.*, 25.

³² *Ibid.*, 26-30.

³³ *Ibid.*, 32.

³⁴ *Ibid.*, 33-37.

³⁵ *Ibid.*, 42.

³⁶ *Ibid.*, 75. Also 47-49.

³⁷ *Ibid.*, 59.

³⁸ *Ibid.*, 77-78, 7.

³⁹ *Ibid.*, 80, 82.

⁴⁰ *Ibid.*, 83-94, 90. For additional information on the treatment of ambassadors, see Rycaut, *The History of the Turkish Empire from the Year 1623 to the Year 1677*, p. 20.

⁴¹ Rycaut, 97-105, 97.

⁴² Rycaut, 90, 158-62.

⁴³ Rycaut, 90, 158-62, 166-68. Ch. XXVI, "Of their Morality, Good Works, and some certain of their Laws worthy of observation."

⁴⁴ Rycaut, 169-173. Also 174-181. "A Computation of the Numbers of the Forces arising from the Zaims and Timariots."

⁴⁵ The question of military strength raises that of Rycaut's sources and point of view. Sonia Anderson states that Rycaut had access to good sources. In particular she cites his information on the strength of Ottoman forces around Buda, acquired there as he travelled through to Vienna in 1665-1666, with the manuscript of *The Present State* in his luggage. The information so acquired was a ". . . military secret of no small importance" (See "Sir Paul Rycaut, F.R.S.") or a "jornalistic coup" (See Paul Rycaut and his Journey . . ."). Since most of the figures in the chapter, building up to the figure 83,380, came from Anatolian "registers", the figures from Buda, on his page 180, might be viewed as a journalistic coup, especially in the sense of a last minute addition to a work on its way to publication. But that there were any military secrets involved seems most unlikely; Metin Kunt's important work, *The Sevants of the Sultan*, p. 80, p. 101, gives information about the kinds of materials, in copies, generally archaic and inaccurate, that might have come into foreigners' hands. In any event, although Rycaut hints at signs of weakness in the system, the timar system as he described it was a thing of the sixteenth

century. See Shaw, 172-174, for manifestations of decline not evident to Rycaut. Rycaut correctly cited the reign of Sultan Süleyman as the high point in the strength of the timar system, and on 203-204 emphasized the importance to the Ottomans of the large numbers of "segbans" and "sarigias" in the Ottoman army.

46 Rycaut, 190, 199.

47 *Ibid.*, 210-212.

48 *Ibid.*, 206.

49 *Ibid.*, 217-218.

50 See Bibliography under Rycaut for the original, anonymous version. Also Rycaut's *The Counterfeit Messiah, or False Christ of the Jews at Smyrna in the Year 1666. . . .,* pp. 13. 30.

51 *The Philosophical Transactions of the Royal Society* (1809), #20, p. 360.

52 *The Correspondence of Henry Oldenbourg,* IV, 606-607. Rycaut's answers seem to have been sketchy and incomplete. He did not identify his sources, but he did recommend the bearer of his letter, Pietro Cesi, as a "great traveller and rarely well versed in the Arabick and Turkish languages." The Society voted Cesi its thanks for the letter and for 36 unspecified curiosities he had brought with him. Cesi then joined Bobowski in the shadows. See Thomas Birch, *History of the Royal Society,* II, 212; *Diary of John Evelyn,* III, 522.

53 Paul Rycaut, *The History of the Present State of the Greek and Armenian Churches,* Preface.

54 *Ibid.*, 330.

55 *Ibid.*, 339-355.

56 *Ibid.*, 355-358.

57 *Ibid.*, 397.

58 Anderson, 478.

59 Paul Rycaut, "The Memoirs . . ." in *The History of the Turkish Empire From the Year 1623 . . .* 131, 140, "The Proceedings of the War in Hungary", 140-146.

60 Paul Rycaut, "The Reign of Sultan Mehmet . . .", in *The Turkish History From the Year 1623 . . .* 165.

61 *Ibid.*, The History of the Famous Siege of Candia", 195-207, 211.

62 *Ibid.*, 224.

63 *Ibid.*, 251, 256. The structure at Izmir was said to have been constructed with stones taken from classical ruins. Rycaut said he agreed with Ahmet Köprülü, that nothing must stand in the way of commerce. See *The Present State of the Greek and Armenian Churches,* 35-37.

64 Anderson, 478.

65 *The Diary of Samuel Pepys,* Vol. VI, 21-22 (October 25, 1666), 218 (March 20-21, 1666), 248 (April 7-9, 1667), 256 (April 12-13, 1667), 286 (May 3-5, 1667).

Chapter 6

1 A. C. Wood, *History of the Levant Company,* p. 130.

2 Thomas Smith, *Remarks Upon the Manners, Religion, and Government of the Turks . . .* (1678).

3 John Covel, "Extracts from the Diaries of John Covel, 1670-1679," in *Early Voyages and Travels in the Levant,* ed. J. T. Dent (1893), p. 140.

[4] *Ibid.*, 166.

[5] *Ibid.*, 184.

[6] *Ibid.*, 185.

[7] *Ibid.*, 195.

[8] *Ibid.*, 199-201.

[9] *Ibid.*, 208.

[10] *Ibid.*, 213.

[11] *Ibid.*, 239.

[12] *Ibid.*, 247.

[13] Roger North, *The Lives of the Right Honourable Francis North.* . . . etc. (1890), 34-35, 51-64, 84-87. See also Anderson, *op. cit.*, 275 and H. Bowen, *British Contributions to Turkish Studies,* 17.

[14] Paul Rycaut, *The History of the Turks Beginning with the Year 1679* (London: Clabell, 1700), 1-12. See also Abbott, 194.

[15] Rycaut, *op. cit.*, 18.

[16] *Ibid.*, 21-27.

[17] Paul Rycaut, *The Turkish History* (London: Isaac Cleave, 1704), 313. In 1681 Rycaut had published a translation of Baltazar Gracian's *The Critick* which he had done much earlier. There he had argued that the Ottoman ascent to power had been too sudden and too violent to endure. Their sudden rise left the Ottomans blind to their own weaknesses. See Rycaut, *The Critick,* (London, 1681), 73, 151, 207.

[18] Hatton, *Europe in the Age of Louis XIV,* 78-79. See also John Lough, *France Observed in the Seventeenth Century by English Travelers* (1985), 133, 142 for English accounts and descriptions of the French monarchy which recalled descriptions given of the Ottoman state. For example: "The government of the King is merely, and indeed regal, or to give it the true name, *despoticall*" (Peter Heylyn, 1656) and "The French kings have a most absolute power" (Sir John Reresby, 1650).

[19] Daniel Defoe, *An Appeal to Honour and Justice* (1715), 51.

[20] Daniel Defoe, *Defoe's Reviews,* Vol. I, no. 55 p. 234. (September 12, 1704).

[21] *Ibid.*, no. 56, pp. 237-239 (Sept. 16, 1704; no. 77, pp. 321-322 (November 26, 1704).

[22] Paul Cernovodeanu, "The General Condition of the English Trade. . . ." *Revue des études sud-est européens* V (1967), 458-460.

[23] Paul Cernovodeanu, "England and the Question of Free Trade in the Black Sea. . . .", *Revue roumaine d'histoire,* V (1967), 20-21. See also Bruce McGowan, *Economic Life in Ottoman Europe,* 71.

[24] Rifa'at A. Abou el Haj, "Ottoman Diplomacy at Karlowitz," *Journal of the American Oriental Society,* LXXXVII (1967), 498.

[25] Sir Edward S. Creasy, *History of the Ottoman Turks,* 318; also el Haj, 502-510; L. V. Thomas and N. Itzokowitz, *A Study of Naima,* 57, 90.

[26] Act IV, Scene 1.

[27] *Letters Writ by a Turkish Spy,* ed. A. J. Weitzman, p. xiii.

[28] G. A. Grelot, *Description of a Late Voyage to Constantinople* (1683), p. 2. See Halil Inalcik, *The Ottoman Empire. The Classical Age* for a serene drawing of Topkapi from this work. See C. G. Cox *A Reference Guide to the Literature of Travel,* 1933, 213-214.

[29] Jean Thévenot, *The Travels of Monsieur de Thévenot.* . . . (1687), 29-37.

[30] *Ibid.*, 57.

[31] *Ibid.*, 59, 81.

[32] du Vigneau, *A New Account of the Present Condition of Turkish Affairs with the Causes of the Decay of the Ottoman Power* (London, B. Taylor, 1688), 11.

[33] *Ibid.*, 118.

[34] Thomas Smith, "An Account of the City of Brusa in Bythnia . . ." in *A Collection of Curious Travels and Voyages*, ed. John Ray (London, 1693), 50-90.

[35] Thomas Vaughan, *A Grammar of the Turkish Language* (1709) (reprint, The Scolar Press, 1968; see Publisher's Note.) The first Turkish grammar in the Western world was H. Magiser's *Institutionum linguae Turcicae* (1612). Andre du Ryer followed with the *Rudimenta grammatices linguae Turcicae* (1630). Third on the list of pioneers is G. Molino, author of *Dittionario delle lingua Italiana, Turchesca* (1641). That work was superseded by M. Meninski's *Thesaurus linguarum Orientalum Turicae* (1680). Paul Rycaut had recommended the study of Turkish in *The Turkish History*, vol. II, p. 20. William Seaman's *Grammaticae et linguae Turchicae* appeared again in 1773 (London: H. Hall). See also Bowen, 22-23; Dereli, 33; Moran 54.

[36] Thomas Vaughan, *op. cit.*, "Preface."

[37] Aaron Hill, *A Full and Just Account of the Present State of the Ottoman Empire* (London, 1710), 37.

[38] *Ibid.*, 76.

Conclusion

[1] M. A. Cook, *A History of the Ottoman Empire to 1730*, p. 1.

[2] Richard Knolles, *The Generall Historie of the Turkes . . . with a New Continuation . . .* (1638), "A Brief Discourse. . . ."

[3] Metin I. Kunt, *op. cit.*, pp. 35, 40-41. Also for the decline of the *devşirme* and the Palace School, see H. A. R. Gibb and H. Bowen, *Islamic Society and the West* (1957), Vol. I. 81 n; Lewis Thomas, pp. 22-25. For routes of entry into the Ottoman ruling class—volunteers from the subject classes, sons and heirs of Ottomans, and men from the households and retinues of Ottomans—see Metin Kunt, 35 *et passim*.

[4] Lewis Thomas, 122.

[5] *Ibid.*, 65-6, 77-83.

[6] Norman Itzkowitz, *Ottoman Empire*, p. 103.

[7] Michael Levy, *The World of Ottoman Art*, ch. v. Also Shaw, 234-238.

[8] H. S. Bennett, *English Books and Readers, 1475-1557*, 135, quoting from the *Short Title Catalogue* no, 5734 Air.

Bibliographies

Primary Sources

Abercromby, D.: *The Present State of the Ottoman Empire.* . . . London, 1660.

Ahmad I, Sultan: *Letters from the Great Turke.* Amsterdam: Theatrum Orbis Terrarum Ltd., Da Capo Press, 1971.

Anonymous: *Newes from Turkie and Poland. Or a true and compendious declaration of the Proceedings between the Great Turke and his Majesty of Poland, from the beginning of the Warres untill the latter end.* London, 1622.

————: *A True and Faithfull Relation of What Hath Lately Happened in Constantinople Concerning the Death of the Sultan Osman, and the Setting up of Mustafa his Uncle.* London, 1622.

————: *A Wilderness. The Present State of the Ottoman Empire.* London, 1670.

————: *The Strangling and Death of the great Turke and his two sonnes. With the strange preservation and deliverance of his uncle Mustafa from perishing in Prison.* London, 1622.

————: *The Turkes Secretarie, Containing his sundry Letters.* . . . London: M. B., 1607.

————: *Letters Writ by a Turkish Spy.* London, 1687-1694. See Marana, Giovanni Paolo, *infra.*

————: *True Copies of the insollent, cruell . . . letter lately written by the great Turke for denouncing of Warre against the King of Poland: And of the answere made by the said King.* London: 1621.

Ascham, Roger: *English Works.* W. A. Wright, ed. Cambridge: Cambridge University Press, 1970.

Aubrey, John: *Aubrey's Brief Lives,* O. L. Dick, ed. Ann Arbor: University of Michigan Press, 1957.

Bacon, Francis: "Of the True Greatness of Kingdoms and Estates." *Essays* (1597-1635), no. 29. New York: Walter J. Black, 1942.

Barrow, Isaac: *The Works of Isaac Barrow, D. D.* New York: John C. Riker, 1845. 3 vol. Vol. III contains: "Epitome Fidei et Religionis Turcicae" (pp. 398-407) and "De Religione Turcica" (pp. 511-519).

Baudier, Michel: *Histoire generalle du Serrail et de la cour du Gand Seigneur Empereur des Turcs . . . ensemble, l'histoire de le cour du Roy de la Chine.* Paris: 1626.

————: *The History of the Imperiall Estate of the Grand Seigneur: Their Habitations, Lives, Titles, Qualities, Exercises, Workes, Revenues, Habit, Discent, Ceremonies, Magnificence, Judgements, Officers, Favourites, Religion, Power, Government and*

Tyranny. Translated out of the French by E.G.S.A. [Edward Grimestone, Serjant at Arms] London: William Stansky, 1633.

Bent, J. Theodore: ed. *Early Voyages and Travels in the Levant.* I. *The diary of Master Thomas Dallam, 1599-1600.* II. *Extracts from the diaries of Dr. John Covel, 1670-1679; with some account of the Levant Company of Turkey merchants.* London: Hakluyt Society, 1893.

Bibliander, Theodorus: *A Godly Consultation unto the Brethren and Companyons of the Christen Religion. By What Meanes the Cruell Power of the Turkes bothe may and ought to be Repelled of the Christen People.* Basel: R. Bonifante, 1542.

Biddulph, William: *The Travels of certaine Englishmen into Africa, Asia, Troy, Bythnia, Thracia, and to the Blacke Sea . . .* London: W. Aspley, 1609.

————: *The travels of Foure English men & a preacher . . . begonne in the yeere of Iubile, 1600 . . .* London: W. Aspley, 1612.

————: *The Travels of Foure Englishmen and a Preacher.* London: T. Lavender, 1612.

Billerbeg, Frauncis: *Most rare and strange Discourses of Amurath the Turkish Emperour that now is. Of his personne and how he is governed; with the warres between him and the Persians, and also of the Tartars and the Moscouites; of the Peace concluded between King Phillip and the great Turke: The Turkish triumph . . . with the Confession of the Patriarke of Constantinople, exhibited to the great Turke. . . .* London: I. Hackett, 1585.

Birch, Thomas: *History of the Royal Society of London.* London, 1756-1757. New York: Johnson Reprints, 1968. 4 vols.

[Blount, Sir Henry]: *A Voyage into the Levant. A Briefe Relation of a Journey Lately Performed by Master H. B., Gentleman, from England, by way of Venice, into Dalmatia, Sclavonia, Bosnah, Hungary, Macedonia, Thessaly, Thrace, Rhodes, Egypt, unto Gran Cairo. With particular observations concerning the moderne condition of the Turkes, and other people under that Empire.* London: A. Crooke, 1636.

Bobovi, Albert: *Mémoirs sur les Turc.* Constantinople, Nov. 10, 1666. Paul Riant Collection, Harvard, Ott. 3030.4

————: "A Treatise of Bobovius, sometime first interpreter to Mohamet III, concerning the liturgy of the Turks, their Pilgrimage to Mecca, their circumcision, Visitation of the Sick," in Anon., *Four Treatises Concerning the Doctrine, Discipline, and Worship of the Mahometanes.* London: J. Darby, 1712.

———— (Bobowski): *Serei endurum das ist: Inwendige Beschaffenheit der Türckischen Kaysere: Residenz zu Constantinopoli; die neue Burg gennant/samt dero Ordnung und Gebrauchen/so von Alberto Bobovio Leopoltano/welcher zur Zeit der strangulierten Kaysere Ibrahim/auch jetzt noch regierenden Sultan Mehmet/daselbst für einen Peygen der Muste etliche Jahr lang gedien und in italienischer Sprach beschrieben hatte.* N. Brenner, transl. Vienna, 1667.

Bodin, Jean: *The Six Bookes of a Commonweale.* Richard Knolles, transl. London: G. Bishop, 1606. (Facsimile reprint, ed. K. D. McRae. Cambridge: Harvard University Press, 1962).

————: *Six Books of the Commonwealth,* transl. by M. J. Tooley. Oxford: Blackwell, n.d.

————: *Colloquium of the Seven About Secrets of the Sublime,* transl. by Marion Kuntz. Princeton: Princeton University Press, 1975.

124

Bon, Ottaviano: *A Brief Discourse of the most Assured Ways and Means to pull down and ruine the vast monarchy of the Ottoman Princes.* London, 1687.

———: *A Description of the Grand Signor's Seraglio, or Turkish Emperours Court.* London: J. Ridley, 1650. [See N. Penzer, *The Harem* n.d., p. 35 for information on the history of this work in translation.]

Botero, Giovanni: *Relations of the Most Famous Kingdoms and Commonwealth Through the World.* London: John Iaggard, 1608.

———: *Relations of the most famous kingdomes and common weales thorowout the world: discoursing of their situation, religion, language, manners, customs, strengths, greatnesse, and policies. Translated out the best Italian impression of Boterus. And since the last edition by R. J., now once again enlarged according to moderne observation with additions of new states and countries.* London: John Haviland, 1630.

———: *The Traveller's Breviat, or an historical description of the most famous kingdomes in the world,* transl. R. Johnson. London: Bollifante, 1601.

Burbury, John: *A Relation of a Journey of the Right Honourable My Lord Henry Howard from London to Vienna and thence to Constantinople in the Company of his Excellency Count Lesley. . . .* London: T. Collins, 1671.

Burian, Orhan: *Babaali Nezdinde Üçüncü Ingliz Elcisi Lello 'nun Muhtirasi.* Ankara: Turk Kurumu Basimevi, 1952.

Busbecq, Ogier Ghislain de: *Letters of Ogier Ghislain de Busbecq to the Holy Roman Emperor Maximilian II.* Newly translated and edited from the Latin text of J. B. Howaert, Brussels, 1632. Ed. by R. E. Jones and B. C. Weber. New York: Bookman Associates, 1961.

———: *The Four Epistles of A. G. Busbecquius concerning his embassy into Turkey, being remarks upon the religion, customs, riches, strengths and government of that people: As also a description of their chief cities and places of trade and commerce. To which is added his advice on how to manage war against the Turks.* Done into English. London: J. Taylor and J. Wyat, 1694.

———: *The Turkish Letters of Ogier Ghiselin de Busbecq.* Translated from the Elzevir ed. of 1633 by E. S. Forster. Oxford: Claredon Press, 1927, 1968.

Cambini, Andrea: *Two Commentaries. The One of the Originall of the Turks. The Other of the Warre of the Turks Against George Scanderberg.* Amsterdam: Theatrum Orbis Terrarum Ltd. Da Capo Press, 1976.

———: *Two very notable commentaries one the originall of the Turkes . . . the other of the warres . . . of George Scanderberg,* tr. J. Shute. London: R. Hall, 1562.

Campbell, Lilly, ed.: *Mirrour for Magistrates* (1559). Cambridge: Cambridge University Press, 1938; New York; Barnes & Noble, 1960.

Carr, Ralph: *The Mahumetane or Turkish Historie . . . translated from the French and Italian tongues by R. Carr.* London: T. Este, 1600.

Cartwright, John: *The Preacher's travels . . . and a briefe rehearsall of some gross absurdities in the Turkish Alcoran.* London: T. Thorpe, 1611.

Chishull, Edmund: *Travels in Turkey and back to England.* London W. Bowyer 1747.

Castlemaine, Roger Palmer: *An Account of the Present War between the Venetians and Turkes; with the state of Candie.* London: H. Herringman, 1666.

Chassepol, Francois de: *The History of the Grand Viziers, Mahomet and Achmet Caprogli, of the Three Last Signiors, their Sultana's and Chief Favourites . . . Englished by John Evelyn, Junior.* London: H. Brome, 1677.

125

Covel, John: *Autograph Journals of Dr. John Covel during his travels in Asia Minor, Greece, Switzerland, Italy, and France.* British Museum, Add. MS. 22914.

————: "Extracts from the Diaries of John Covel, 1670-1679," in *Early Voyages and Travels in the Levant,* ed. J. T. Bent. London: Hakluyt Society, 1893.

Dallam, Thomas: "The Diary of Master Thomas Dallam, 1599-1690," in *Ibid.*

Defoe, Daniel: *An Appeal to Honour and Justice.* London: J. Baker, 1715

————, *Defoe's Review, 1704-1713.* New York: Columbia University Press for Facsimile Text Society, 1938. 9 vols. Especially Vol. I: #53, September 12, 1704, #56, September 16, 1704, and #77, November 26, 1704.

Dumont, Jean: *A New Voyage to the Levant, Containing an Account of the Most Remarkable Curiosities in Germany, France, Italy, Malta, and Turkey.* London: M. Gilliflower, 1696.

Erasmus, Desiderius: *The Enchiridion,* ed. and transl. by R. Himelick. Bloomington: Indiana University Press, 1963.

————: *The Praise of Folly,* H. W. van Loon, ed. New York: W. and J. Black, 1947.

Evelyn, John: *The Diary of John Evelyn.* Vol. III, E. S. de Beer, ed. London: Bickers and Son, 1879.

Evliya Efendi (Evliya Celebi): *Narrative of Travels in Europe, Asia, and Africa in the Seventeenth Century,* transl. by J. von Hammer-Purgstall. London, 1834; also New York: Johnson Reprint Corporation, 1968.

Finch, Allan George: *Report on the Manuscripts of Allan George Finch, Esg.* Vol. I. London: H. M. Stationery Office, 1913.

Finet, John: *The Beginning, Continuance, and Decay of Estates.* London: J. Brill, 1606.

Fox. *Mr. Harrie Cavendish, His Journey to and from Constantinople in 1689, by his manservant Fox.* A. C. Wood, ed. London: Offices of the Royal Historical Society, 1940.

Gainsford, Thomas: *The Glory of England. Or a True Description of many excellent prerogatives and remarkable blessings whereby she triumpeth over all the Nations in the World. With justifiable comparison betweene herself and the eminent Kingdomes of the Earth plainly manifesting the defects of them all* . . . . London: R. Whittakers, 1619. [Pages from the edition of 1618 may be found in R. C. Temple ed., *The Travels of Peter Mundy,* Cambridge: The Hakluyt Society, vol. I (1907).]

Georgievich, Bartolomaeo *De Turcarum Rite et Ceremoniis* . . . Antverpiae: Georgium Bontium 1544.

————, *De Turcarum moribus epitome* Lugduni: Ioan Tornaesium, 1555.

Geuffroy, Antoine: *The Order of the Great Turkes, of hys menne of warre, and of all hys conquestes, with the summe of Mahumetane Doctryne.* R. Grafton, transl. London, 1542. [on cover, 1524]

Giovio, Paolo: *Short Treatise of the Turks Chronicles compiled by Paulus Govius dedicated to Charles the 6. Emperour and translated out of Latyn into English by Peter Ashton.* London, 1546

Goffe, Thomas: *Courageous Turk and Raging Turk.* Oxford: The Malone Society Reprints, University Press, 1974. Contains: "The Raging Turk, or, Baiazet the Second," and "The Courageous Turke, or, Amurath the First", 1631.

Gough, Hugh tr: *The Offspring of the House of Ottomano, and officers pertaining to the Great Turkes Court; Whereunto is Added Barthdomaeus Georgieviz Epitome, of the costumes, Rytes, Ceremonies, and Religion of the Turkes; with the miserable afflictions of these Christians whiche live under their captivitie and bondage.* London: T. Marshe, 1570 (?).

Greaves, John: *A Description of the Grand Signour's Seraglio or the Turkish Emperour's Palace.* London: J. Martin, 1650.

Grelot, Guillaumẹ Joseph: *A Late Voyage To Constantinople. Containing An Exact Description of the Propontis and Hellespont, with the Dardanels . . . as also of the City of Constantinople. . . . Made English by J. Philips.* London: J. Playford and H. Bonwicke, 1683.

Harff, Arnold von: *The Pilgrimage of Arnold von Harff, Knight.* London: Hakluyt Society, 1946.

Hakluyt, Richard, comp.: *The Principall Navigations, Voyages, Traffiques, and Discoveries of the English Nation.* London: G. Bishop, 1589. Also London: J. M. Dent & Sons, 1927-1928. Facsimile edition, Cambridge University Press for the Hakluyt Society, 1965. 2 vols.

Harris, John: *Itinerarium Bibliotheca, or, A Complete Collection of Voyages and Travels. . . .* London: T. Wood. . . . 1744. (First edition, 1705). 2 Vols, quarto. Vol. II, Book iii: *Voyages and Travels through the Dominions of the Grand Signior. . . .*

Harrison, G. B., ed.: *The Elizabethan Journals, Being a Record of Those Things Most Talked About During the Years 1571 to 1597* [in Vol. I] *and 1598-1603* [in Vol. II]. Garden City: Doubleday, 1965.

Higgons, Thomas: *The History of Issuef Bassa, Captain General of the Ottoman Army at the Invasion of Candia.* London: R. Kettlewell, 1684.

Hill, Aaron: *A Full and Just Account of the Present State of the Ottoman Empire in all its Branches. . . .* London: J. Mayo, 1710.

Holwel, John: *An Appendix to Holwel's Catastrophe Mundi, being an Astrological Discourse of the Rise, Growth, and Continuation of the Othoman Family.* London: F. Smith, 1683.

Hughes, Charles, ed.: *Shakespeare's Europe: A Survey of Europe at the End of the Sixteenth Century, being Unpublished Chapters of Fynes Maryson's Itinerary, 1617.* New York: Benjamin Blom 1967.

Hutton, Charles, Shaw, G., and Pearson, R., eds.: *The Philosophical Transactions of the Royal Society of London from their Commencement in 1685 to the year 1800.* London: C. R. Baldwin, 1809.

Knolles, Richard: *The Generall Historie of the Turkes, from the first beginning of that Nation to the rising of the Othoman Familie, with all the notable Expeditions of the Christian Princes against them, together with the Lives and Conquests of the Ottoman Kings and Emperours; faithfullie collected out of the best Histories, both auntient and moderne, and digested into one continual Historie until this present yeare 1603.* London: A Islip, 1603.

————: *Same With a new continuation from the yeare of our Lord 1629 unto the yeare 1638 faithfully collected.* London: Adam Islip, 1638.

————: *Same With a Continuation to this Present Year 1687. Whereunto is Added the Present State of the Ottoman Empire. By Sir Paul Rycaut, late consul of Smyrna.* The Sixth Edition. . . . London: Thomas Basset 1687.

————: *The Turkish History. Comprehending the Origin of that Nation. And the Growth of the Ottoman Empire. Written by Mr. Knolles, and Continued by the Honourable Sir Paul Rycaut, to 1699. And abridged by Mr. Savage.* London: I. Cleave, 1701.

127

Kreutel, R. F., ed.: *Leben und Taten der türkischen Kaiser. Die anonyme vulgär-griechische Chronik.* Graz: Verlag Styria, 1971.

Lachmann, Renate, ed.: *Memoiren eines Janitscharen, oder Türkische Chronik.* Graz: Verlag Styria, 1975.

Lavardin, Jacques: *The Historie of George Castriot, Surnamed Scanderbeg, King of Albanie, Containing his famous actes, his noble deeds of Armes, and memorable victories against the Turkes, for the Faith of Christ. . . . newly translated out of French into English by Z. J.* [Zachary Jones], *Gentleman.* London: H. Ponsonby, 1590.

Lithgow, William: *A Most Delectable and true discourse of an admired and painful peregrination from Scotland to the most famous Kingdomes in Europe, Asia, Affrike, etc.* London, Oakes, 1623.

————: *The Rare Adventures of William Lithgow.* Glasgow: W. Maclehose, 1632.

Lonicerus, Philip. *Chronicorum Turcicorum. Tomus Primus.* Frankfurt, 1520.

Löwenclau, J. (Leunclavius): "Annales sultanorum othmanidorum sua lingua scripta," and "Pandectes historia turcicae," Frankfurt, 1590. In V. Migne, *Patrologia Graeca,* Paris, 1866.

————: *Historiae Musulmanae Turcorum.* Frankfurt: A. Wechel, 1591.

————: *Neuwer Musulmanischer Historie . . .* Frankfurt: J. Aubry, 1590.

R. M.: *Learne of a Turke; or instructions and advise sent from the Turkish army at Constantinople to the English army at London.* London: 1660.

Machiavelli, Nicolo: *The Chief Works and Others,* Alan Gilbert, ed. Durham: Duke University Press, 1965.

McLaughlin, M. M. and Ross, J. B., comp.: *The Portable Medieval Reader.* New York: Viking Press, 1972.

Marana, Giovanni Paolo: *Letters Writ by a Turkish Spy,* ed. Arthur J. Weitzman. New York: Columbia University Press, 1970.

Marsh, W.: *A New Survey of the Turkish Empire and Government. . . . with their Laws, Religion and Customs.* London, 1663.

Minadoi, Tomasso: *The history of the warres between the Turks and the Persians,* A. Hartwell, tr. London: J. Wolfe, 1595.

Moore, Andrew: *A Compendious History of the Turks. Containing an exact Account of the Originall of that People: the Rise of the Othoman Familie; and the Valiant Undertakings of the Christian Princes Against Them: With their Various Events.* London: J. Streater, 1660.

Moryson, Fynes: *An Itinerary, containing his ten years travell through the twelve dominions of Germany, Bohmerland, Switzerland, Netherland, Denmarke, Poland, Italy, Turkey, France, England, Scotland, Ireland.* London, 1617. Glasgow, J. Maclehose, 1907.

Mundy, Peter: *The Travels sof Peter Mundy in Europe and Asia, 1608-1667.* Volume I: *Travels in Europe & Asia 1608-1628.* ed. R. C. Temple. Cambridge: Hakluyt Society, Second Series, 1907.

Münster, Sebastian: *A briefe collection and compendious extract of straunge and memorable things gathered out of the Cosmographye of Sebastian Münster.* London: T. Marsh, 1574.

Newton, Thomas: *A Notable History of the Saracens.* London: H. Row, 1575.

Nicolay, Nicolas de: *The Navigations, peregrinations and voyages Made into Turkie by*

128

Nicholas Nicholay Daulphinois . . . T. Washington, tr. London: T. Dawson, 1585. Also London: T. Osborne, 1745.

Nixon, Anthony: *The Three English Brothers. Sir Thomas Sherley his travels, with his three years imprisonment in Turkey.* . . . *Sir Anthony Sherley, his embassage to the Christian Princes. Master Robert Sherley his warres against the Turkes.* . . . London: J. Hodgetts, 1607.

North, Roger: *The Lives of the Right Honourable Francis North, Baron Guilford, the Honourable Sir Dudley North and the Honourable and Reverend Dr. John North.* A. Jessopp, ed. London: G. Bell & Sons, 1890.

Oldenbourg, Henry: *The Correspondence of Sir Henry Oldenbourg.* A. R. Hall and M. B. Hall, eds. Madison: University of Wisconsin Press, 1965. Six volumes.

Osborne, Francis: *Political Reflections Upon the Government of the Turks.* London: T. Robinson, 1656.

Pepys, Samuel: *The Diary of Samuel Pepys,* H. B. Wheatley, ed. London: G. Bell, 1923.

Perrot, John: *Blessed openings of a day of good things to the Turks.* London: T. Simon, 1658.

————: *A Visitation of Love, and gentle greeting of the Turk and tender tryal of his thoughts for God, and proof of the hearts of his Court.* London: T. Simon, 1684.

Peter, John: *A Relation or Diary of the Siege of Vienna.* London: W. Nott, 1684.

Pius II, Pope (Sylvio Piccolomini): "A Call for Common Action against the Turks." In: *The Portable Medieval Reader,* ed. J. B. Ross and M. M. McLaughlin. New York: Viking Press. Pp. 319-321.

Préchac, Jean de: *The Grand Vizier, or the History of the Life of Cara Mustafa who commanded the Turkish Army at the Siege of Vienna in 1683. Containing his Rise, his Amours in the Seraglio, and the true reason of his undertaking the Siege of Vienna, with the Particulars of his Death at Belgrade.* London: H. Hill, 1685.

————: *The Serasquier Pasha: An Historical Novel of the Times. Containing all that pass'd at the Siege of Buda. Out of the French.* London: H. Rhodes, 1685.

Purchas, Samuel: *Hakluytus Posthumus, or Purchas His Pilgrimes.* Glasgow: J. Maclehose & Sons, 1905. Vol. VIII contains: "A Relation of a Journey Begun Anno Dom. 1610, Written by Master George Sandys, and here contracted" (pp. 88-247); "Part of a Letter of Master William Biddulph from Aleppo" (pp. 248-314); "The Journal of Edward Barton, Esq., Her Majesties Ambassador with the Grand Signor, otherwise called the Great Turke, in Constantinople, Sultan Mahomet Chan. Written by Sir Thomas Glover. . . ." "Two Letters . . . by the same Ambassador Barton" (pp. 304-320); "The Travels and Adventures of Captain John Smith in divers parts of the World, begun about the yeare 1596" (pp. 321-342); "The Death of Sultan Osman and the setting up of Mustafa his Uncle, according to the Relation presented to her Majestie" (pp. 343-359).

Vol. IX contains: "The Grand Signor's Seraglio (Robert Withers)" (pp. 321-406; ". . . A Letter sent by Sultan Osman to his Majestie . . . " (pp. 407-409); "The . . . Letter by Halil Bashaw to Sir Paul Pindar . . ." (pp. 409-411); "Sundrie the personall voyages performed by John Sanderson of London, Merchant, begun in October, 1581, Ended in October, 1602. With an historicall Description of Constantinople" (pp. 412-486); "Two Letters of M. John Nuberry . . . with three other letters from M. Eldred . . . found amongst the papers of M. William Harborne . . . communicated to me by M. John Sanderson" (pp. 493-502).

Vol. X contains: "Master Thomas Coryates Travels to, and Observations in

Constantinople . . ." (pp. 389-447); "Relation of the Travels of W. Lithgow, a Scot . . ." (pp. 447-492): "Later Intelligence Out of Turkie . . . Touching the Resignation of Mustafa (pp 492-499).

Ray, John: *A Collection of Curious Travels and Voyages*. London: R. Southwell, 1693.

Reusner, N.: *Epistolarum Turcicarum Variorum et Diversorum Authorum*. Frankfurt: Moenum, 1595-1660.

Roe, Thomas: *The Negotiations of Sir Thomas Roe in his Embassy to the Ottoman Porte from the Year 1621 to 1628 Inclusive*. London: S. Richardson, 1740.

Rycaut, Paul: *The Capitulations and Articles of Peace . . . betweene . . . the King of England . . . and the Sultan . . . Which Serve Towards the Maintenance of a Well Grounded Peace and Security of Trade and Traffique of his Majestie's Subjects in the Levant*. Istanbul: Abraham Gabai, 1663. [I have not seen this book, which is very rare; Anderson, "Sir Paul Rycaut, F. R. S. . . ." p. 274 knows of only four extant copies.

——— [published anonymously]: *A Narration of the success of the Voyage of the Right Honourable Heneage Finch, Earl of Winchelsea . . . from Smyrna to Constantinople; His Arrival there, the manner of his Entertainment and Audience with the Grand Vizier and Grand Signor*. 1661.

——— [published anonymously]: *History of the Three late famous Imposters, viz., Pedro Ottomano, Mahomet Bei, and Sabatai Sevi*. 1669.

———: *The Critick. Written Originally in Spanish by Lorenzo Gracean, one of the best wits in Spain and Translated into English by Paul Rycaut Esq*. London: Henry Broome, 1681.

———: *The Counterfeit Messiah or False Christ of the Jews at Smyrna in the Year 1666. Written by an English Person of Quality there resident, soon after the affair happened*. Keene, New Hampshire: C. Sturtevant, 1795.

———: *The Present State of the Greek and Armenian Churches*. London: J. Starkoy, 1679. Also New York: AMS Reprints, 1970.

———: *The Present State of the Ottoman Empire. Containing the Maxims of the Turkish Politie, the most Material Points of the Mahometane Religion . . . their military discipline . . . Illustrated with divers pieces of sculpture representing the variety of habits amongst the Turks*. London: J. Starkey, 1668. N.Y.: Ayer, formerly Arno, 1970.

———: *The History of the Turkish Empire from the Year 1623 to the Year 1677. Containing the Lives of the Three Last Emperours . . .* London: J. Starkey, 1680.

———: *The History of the Turks. Beginning with the Year 1679 . . .* R. Clavell & A. Roper. London. 1700.

———: *The Turkish History*. London: I. Cleave, 1704.

——— [Knolles'] *The Turkish History. Volume II: The Turkish History . . . with a Continuation by Sir Paul Rycaut. Vol. III: The History of the Turks beginning with the Year 1679, until the end of the year 1698 and 1699*. London: Thomas Basset, 1687-1700.

——— [Knolles']: *The Turkish Historie . . . continued by . . . Sir Paul Rycaut to the Peace at Carolowitz in 1699, and abridged by Mr. Savage*. London, 1701.

DuRyer, Sieur: *The Alcoran of Mahomet, translated out of Arabique into French by Sieur Du Ryer . . . A needful caveat or admonition for them who desire to know what use may be made, or if there be danger in reading the Alcoran*. London: A. Ross, 1649.

Sanderson, John: *The Travels of John Sanderson in the Levant, 1584-1602.* R. Forster, ed. London: Hakluyt Society, 1931.

Sandys, George: *A Relation of a Journey Begun An: Dom: 1610. Foure Bookes Containing a Description of the Turkish Empire, of Aegypt, of the Holy Land, of the Remote Parts of Italy, and Lands Adjoyning.* London: W. Barrett, 1615.

Schiltberger, Johann: *The Bondage and Travels of Johann Schiltberger . . . 1396-1427.* London: J. B. Telfer, 1879.

Schweigger, Salmon: *Eine neue Reyssbeschreibung aus Teutschlan nach Konstantinopel und Jerusalem . . .* Nürnberg, 1613.

Seaman, William: *Domini nostri Iesu Christi Testamentum Novum, turcice redditum.* Oxon.; 1666.

————: *Grammatica Linguae Turcicae.* Oxon.: H. Hall, 1670.

————: *The Reign of Sultan Orchan Second King of the Turks. Translated out of Hojah Efendi an Eminent Turkish Historian, by William Seaman.* London: T. R. and E. M., 1652.

Shakespeare, William. *The Annotated Shakespeare.* A. L. Rowse, ed. New York: Clarkson N. Potter, 1978.

Sherley, Sir Thomas: *Discoùrs of the Turks.* London: Royal Historical Society, 1936.

Smith, John: *The True Travels, Adventures, and Observations of Captain John Smith in Europe, Asia, Affrica, and America from Anno Domini 1593 to 1629. His Accidents and Sea-Fights in the Straights, his Service and Stratagems of War . . . his three single combats betwixt the Christian Armie and the Turkes. And how he was taken prisoner by the Turks, sold for a slave . . . how he slew the Bashaw . . . and escaped from the Turkes and Tartars.* London: J. H., 1630.

Smith, Thomas: *Remarks Upon the Manners, Religion, and Government of the Turks Together with a Survey of the Seven Churches of Asia as they now lye in their ruines, and a Brief Description of Constantinople.* London: M. Pitt, 1677.

Smythe, Sir John: *Instructions, observations and Orders Militarie.* London: Richard Johns, 1595.

Soranzo, Lazaro: *The Ottomano of Lazaro Soranzo.* A. Hartwell, tr. London: John Windet, 1603.

Tavernier, Jean Baptiste: *Collection of Travels Through Turky into Persia and the East Indies . . .* London: M. P., 1688.

Taylor, John: *A valourous and perillous sea-fight with three, Turkish ships . . . on the Coast of Cornwall . . . .* London: E. Purslow, 1640.

Thévenot, Jean de: *The Travels of Monsieur de Thévenot into the Levant. In Three Parts . . . Newly Done out of French.* London: H. Clark, 1687.

Valle, Pietro della: *Pietro's Pilgrimage. A Journey to India and Back at the Beginning of the Seventeenth Century.* W. Blunt, ed. London: James Barrie, 1953.

Vaughan, Thomas: *A Grammar of the Turkish Language.* London: J, Humpfreys, 1709. Also Menston: The Scolar Press, 1968.

du Vigneau, M. Sieur des Joanots: *A New Account of the Present Condition of Turkish Affairs, with the Causes of the Decay of the Ottoman Power.* London: R. Taylor, 1688.

Webb, Edward: *The rare and most wonderfull thinges which, Ed. Webbe . . . hath seene and passed in all his troublesome trauils. Wherein is set forth his extreame slauverie sustained many years together in the gallies . . . with the manner of his releasment and coming into England in May Last.* London: W. Wright, 1590.

Windet, John: *The Policy of the Turkish Empire.* London: W. S., 1597.

Withers, Robert: *A Description of the Grand Signor's Seraglio. Or Relations of the World and all Religions Observed in all Ages and Places discovered from the Creation, unto this Present.* London, 1620.

———: *A Description of the Grand Signor's Seraglio or Turkish Emperour's Court.* London, 1650.

Worde, W. de: *Here begynnethe a lytell treatyse of the turkes lawe called Alcaron. And also it speketh of Mahamet the Nygromancer.* London, 1515.

Wratislaw of Mitrowitz, Baron Wenceslas: *Adventures: What he Saw in the Turkish Metropolis, Constantinople; experienced in his capitivity; and after his happy return to his Country, committed in writing in the Year of our Lord 1599. Literally translated from the Bohemian by A. R. Wratislaw.* London: Bell and Daddy, 1862.

Secondary Sources

Books

Abbott, C. P.: *Under the Turk in Constantinople. A Record of Sir John Finch's Embassy, 1674-1681*. London: Macmillan, 1920.

Adams, R. P.: *The Better Part of Valor, 1496-1535. More, Erasmus, Colet, Vives on Humanism, War and Peace*. Seattle: University of Washington Press, 1962.

Addison, J. T. *The Christian Approach to the Moslems: An Historical Approach*. New York: AMS Press, 1966.

Alderson, Anthony D.: *The Structure of the Ottoman Dynasty*. Oxford: Clarendon Press, 1956.

Allen, W. E. D.: *Problems of Turkish Power in the Sixteenth Century*. London: Central Asian Research Centre, 1963.

Anderson, Sonia P.: *Paul Rycaut as Consul and Man of Letters at Smyrna (1667-1678)*. Oxford University Diss., 1969.

Arber, Edward, ed.: *An English Garner*. Vol. I. *Voyages and Travels*. Westminster: Constable, 1903.

Atiya, Aziz. *The Crusade in the Later Middle Ages*. London: Methuen, 1938.

———: *The Crusade of Nicopolis*. New York: AMS Press, 1978.

Babinger, Franz: *Die Geschichtsschreiber der Osmanen und ihre Werke*. Leipzig: Harrasowitz, 1927.

———: *Mehmed the Conqueror and His Time*. R. Mannheim, tr., W. C. Hickman, ed., Princeton: Princeton University Press, 1978.

Baker, D., ed.: *Relations between East and West in the Middle Ages*. Edinburgh: Edinburgh University Press, 1973.

Bates, E. S.: *Touring in 1600. A Study of Travel as a Means of Education*. Boston: Houghton Mifflin, 1911.

Beeching, Jack: *The Galleys at Lepanto*. New York: Charles Scribner's Sons, 1982.

Bennett, H. S.: *English Books and Readers, 1475-1557*. Cambridge: Cambridge University Press, 1952.

Bietenholz, P. G.: *Desert and Bedouin in the European Mind: Changing Conceptions from the Middle Ages to the Present Time*. Khartoum: University of Khartoum Extra-Mural Studies Board, 1963.

Bohnstedt, J. W.: *The Infidel Scourge of God: The Turkish Menace as seen by the Pamphleteers of the Reformation Era. Transactions of the American Philosophical Society*, n.s., Vol. LVIII, Part 9.

Bowen, Harold: *British Contributions to Turkish Studies*. London: Longmans Green, 1945.

Brailsford, M. R.: *Quaker Women*. London: Duckworth, 1915.

Braudel, Fernand. *The Mediterranean and the Mediterranean World in the Age of Phillip II*. Sian Reynolds, tr. New York: Harper and Row, 1975.

Brown, Michael J.: *Itinerant Ambassador: the Life of Sir Thomas Roe*. Lexington: University of Kentucky Press, 1970.

Bush, Douglas: *English Literature in the Earlier Seventeenth Century, 1600-1660*. Oxford: Clarendon Press, 1962.

Chew, S. C.: *The Crescent and the Rose: Islam and England During the Renaissance*. New York: Oxford University Press, 1937.

Coles, Paul: *The Ottoman Impact on Europe*. London: Thames and Hudson, 1968.

Cook, M. A., ed.: *Studies in the Economic History of the Middle East from the Rise of Islam to the Present Day*. London: Oxford University Press, 1970.

————: *A History of the Ottoman Empire to 1730*. Cambridge: Cambridge University Press, 1976.

Corbett, J. S.: *England in the Mediterranean: A Study of Rise and Influence of British Power within the Straits*. London: Longmans Green, 1904.

Creasy, Sir Edward S.: *History of the Ottoman Turks*. London: Richard Bentley and Son, 1878.

D'Amico, J. F.: *Renaissance Humanism in Papal Rome. Humanists and Churchmen on the Eve of the Reformation*. Baltimore: The Johns Hopkins University Press, 1983.

Daniel, N. K.: *Islam and the West: The Making of an Image*. Edinburgh: Edinburgh University Press, 1960.

Dannenfeldt, K. H.: *Leonhard Rauwolf. Sixteenth Century Physician, Botanist, and Traveler*. Cambridge: Harvard University Press, 1968.

Davies, D. W.: *Elizabethans Errant. The Strange Fortunes of Sir Thomas Sherley and His Three Sons*. Ithaca: Cornell University Press, 1967.

Davis, Ralph: "England and the Mediterranean," in *Essays on the Economic and Social History of Tudor and Stuart England*, ed. F. J. Fisher. Cambridge: Cambridge University Press, 1974.

Dereli, Hamit: *Kralice Elizabet devrinde Türkler ve Inglizler; bir arastirma*. Istanbul: Anil Maatbasi, 1951.

Ebermann, R.: *Die Türckenfurcht: Ein Beitrag zur Geschichte der öffentlichen Meinung während der Reformationszeit*. Halle an der Saale: C. N. Kaemmerer, 1904.

Elliott, J. H.: *The Old World and the New, 1492-1650*. Cambridge: Cambridge University Press, 1970.

Epstein, M.: *The Early History of the Levant Company*. New York: A. M. Kelley, 1908.

Faroqui, Suraiya: *Town and Townsmen of Ottoman Anatolia. Trade, Crafts, and Food Production in an Urban Setting, 1520-1650*. London: Cambridge University Press, 1984.

Fischer-Galati, S. A.: *Ottoman Imperialism and German Protestantism, 1521-1555*. Cambridge: Harvard University Press, 1959.

Fisher, F. J., ed.: *Essays on the Economic and Social History of Tudor and Stuart England, in Honour of R. H. Tawney*. Cambridge: Cambridge University Press, 1961.

Fisher, Sir Godfrey: *Barbary Legend. War, Trade, and Piracy in North Africa, 1415-1830*. New York: Greenwood Press, 1974.

Fisher, S. N.: *The Foreign Relations of Turkey, 1481-1512*. Urbana: University of Illinois Press, 1948.

Fussner, F. S.: *The Historical Revolution: English Historical Writing and Thought, 1580-1640*. London: Routlege and Kagan Paul, 1962.

Gibb, H. A. R. and Bowen, H.: *Islamic Society and the West: a Study of the Impact of Western Civilization on Moslem Culture in the Near East*. London: Oxford University Press, 1957.

Hale, William, and Bağiş, Ali Ihsan: *Four Centuries of Turco-British Relations. Studies in Diplomatic Economic and Cultural Affairs*. North Humberside: Eothen Press, 1984.

Hammer-Purgstall, Joseph von: *Geschichte des Osmanischen Reiches*. Pest: Hartleben, 1932. Also Graz: Akademische Druck- und Verlagsanstalt, 1963.

Harbage, A., and Schoenbaum, S., eds.: *Annals of English Drama*. Philadelphia: University of Pennsylvania Press, 1964.

Hasluck, F. W.: *Christianity and Islam under the Sultans*. Oxford: Oxford University Press, 1929.

Hatton, R.: *Europe in the Age of Louis XIV*. London: Times and Hudson, 1969.

Hess, Andrew C. *The Forgotten Frontier. A History of the Sixteenth Century Ibero-African Frontier*. Chicago: University of Chicago Press, 1978.

Holt, P. M.: *Studies in the History of the Near East*. London: Frank Cass, 1973.

Horn, D. B.: *British Diplomatic Representatives, 1689-1789*. London: Royal Historical Society, 1932.

————: *The British Diplomatic Service, 1689-1789*. Oxford: Clarendon Press, 1961.

Hurewitz, J. C.: *Diplomacy in the Near and Middle East: A Documentary Record, 1535-1914*. Princeton: van Nostrand, 1956, reprinted 1972.

Inalcik, Halil: *The Ottoman Empire: Conquest, Organization, and Economy. Collected Studies*. London: Variorum Reprints, 1978.

————: *The Ottoman Empire: The Classical Period, 1300-1600*. New York: F. A. Praeger, 1973.

Itzkowitz, N.: *Ottoman Empire and Islamic Tradition*. New York: A. A. Knopf, 1972.

———— and Mote, Max: *Mubadele: An Ottoman-Russian Exchange of Ambassadors*. Chicago: University of Chicago Press, 1970.

Keddie, Nikki R.: *Scholars, Saints, and Sufis. Muslim Religious Institutions Since 1500*. Berkeley: University of California Press, 1972.

Kinross, John Patrick Douglas Balfour, Lord: *The Ottoman Centuries. The Rise and Fall of the Turkish Empire*. New York: William Morrow, 1977.

Kortepeter, C. Max: *Ottoman Imperialism During the Reformation: Europe and the Caucasus*. New York: New York University Press, 1972.

Kunt, I. Metin: *The Sultan's Servants: the Transformation of Ottoman Provincial Government, 1550-1650*. New York: Columbia University Press, 1983.

Kurat, Akdes Nimet: *Türk-Ingliz Münasebetlerinin Başlanğici ve Gelişmesi 1553-1610*. Ankara: Türk Tarih Kurumu Basimevi, 1953.

Lachs, Phyllis: *The Diplomatic Corps Under Charles II and James II*. New Brunswick: Rutgers University Press, 1965.

Lea, H. C.: *The Moriscoes in Spain. Their Conversion and Expulsion*. Philadelphia: Lea Brothers, 1901.

Levy, Michael: *The World of Ottoman Art*. London: Thames and Hudson, 1979.

Lewis, Archibald, ed.: *The Islamic World and the West, 622-1442 A.D.* New York: John Wiley, 1970.

Lewis, Bernard: *Istanbul and the Civilization of the Ottoman Empire.* Norman: Oklahoma University Press, 1963.

———: *The Muslim Discovery of Europe.* New York: W. W. Norton, 1982.

———: *The Middle East and the West.* Bloomington: Indiana University Press, 1964.

——— and Holt, P. M.: *Historians of the Middle East.* London: Oxford University Press, 1962.

Lewis, C. S.: *English Literature of the Sixteenth Century, Excluding Drama.* Oxford: Claredon Press, 1954.

Lewis, W. H.: *Levantine Adventurer. The Travels and Missions of the Chevalier d'Arvieux, 1653-1697.* New York: Harcourt Brace and World, 1957.

Lough, J.: *France Observed in the Seventeenth Century by English Travelers.* Stocksfield: Oriel Press, 1985.

Mantran, R.: "Foreign Merchants and the Minorities in Istanbul in the Sixteenth and Seventeenth Centuries," in *Christians and Jews in the Ottoman Empire: The Functioning of a Plural Society,* ed. by B. Bradel and B. Lewis, pp. 127-137. New York: Holmes and Meier, 1982.

Marshall, P. G. and Williams, Glyndon: *The Great Map of Mankind. Perceptions of New Worlds in the New Age of Enlightenment.* Cambridge: Harvard University Press, 1982.

Mattingly, Garrett: *The Armada.* Boston: Houghton Mifflin, 1959.

———: *Renaissance Diplomacy.* Baltimore: Penguin Books, 1964.

Mayes, Stanley: *An Organ for the Sultan.* London: Putnam Ltd., 1956.

McGowan, Bruce: *Economic Life in Ottoman Europe. Taxation, Trade, and the Struggle for the Land, 1600-1800.* Cambridge: Cambridge University Press, 1981.

McNeill, William H. *Europe's Steppe Frontier. 1500-1600.* Chicago: University of Chicago Press, 1964.

Meienberger, Peter: *John Rudolf Schmid zum Schwarzenhorn als kaiserlicher Resident in Konstantinopel, 1629-43.* Bern: Herbert Lang, 1973.

Metlitzki, Dorothee: *The Matter of Araby in Medieval England.* New Haven: Yale University Press, 1977.

Miller, B.: *Beyond the Sublime Porte: The Grand Seraglio of Stambul.* New Haven: Yale University Press, 1931.

———: *The Palace School of Mahammad the Conqueror.* Cambridge: Harvard University Press, 1941.

Mosse, G. L.: *The Holy Pretense: A Study in Christianity and Reason of State from William Perkins to John Winthrop.* Oxford: Blackwell, 1957.

Mowat, E. B.: *A History of European Diplomacy: 1451-1789.* New York: Longmans, Green, 1928.

Neale, J. M.: *A History of the Holy Eastern Church: the Patriarchate of Alexandria.* London: J. Masters, 1867.

Osmond, P. H.: *Isaac Barrow, His Life and Times.* London: Society for Promoting Christian Knowledge, 1944.

Ozyurt, Senol: *Die Türckenlieder and das Türckenbild in der deutschën Volksüberlieferung vom 16. bis zum 20. Jahrhundert.* München: Wilhelm Fink Verlag, 1972.

Pailin, D. A.: *Attitudes to Other Religions. Comparative Religion in Seventeenth and Eighteenth Century Britain.* Manchester: Manchester University Press, 1984.

Papoulia, B. D.: *Ursprung und Wesen der "Knabenlese" im Osmanischen Reich.* München: Oldenbourg, 1963.

136

Parks, G. B.: *Richard Hakluyt and the English Voyages*. New York: American Geographical Society, 1928.

Parry, V. J.: "Materials of War in the Ottoman Empire," in *Studies in the Economic History of the Middle East from the Rise of Islam to the Present Day*, ed. M. A. Cook. London: Oxford University Press, 1970.

Penrose, Boies: *Urbane Travellers, 1591-1635*. Philadelphia: University of Pennsylvania Press, 1942.

Penzer, N.: *The Harem*. Philadelphia: J. P. Lippincot, n.d.

Pitcher, Donald E.: *A Historical Geography of the Ottoman Empire*. Leiden: E. J. Brill, 1972.

Rawlinson, H. J.: *The Embassy of William Harborne to Constantinople, 1583-1588*. London: Royal Historical Society, 1922.

Read, Conyers: *Mr. Secretary Walsingham and the Policy of Queen Elizabeth*. Oxford: Clarendon Press, 1925.

Refik, Ahmet: *Türkler ve Kralice Elizabet*. Istanbul, 1932.

Ribner, Irving: *The English History Play in the Age of Shakespeare*. Princeton: Princeton University Press, 1957.

Rice, W. G.: *Turk, Moor and Persian in English Literature from 1550 to 1680 with Particular Reference to the Drama*. Diss., Harvard University, 1926.

Rosedale, H. G.: *Queen Elizabeth and the Levant Company*. London: H. Frowde, 1904.

Roth, Cecil: *The House of Nasi. The Duke of Naxos*. New York; Greenwood Press, 1948.

Rouillard, C.: *The Turk in French History, Thought, and Literature, 1520-1660*. Paris, Boivin, 1929.

Rothenberg, G. E.: *The Austrian Military Border in Croatia, 1522-1747*. Urbana: Illinois University Studies in the Social Sciences, Vol. 48, 1960.

Rowland, A. L.: *Studies in English Commerce and Exploration in the Reign of Elizabeth I: England and Turkey: The Rise of Commercial and Diplomatic Relations*. Philadelphia: University of Pennsylvania Press, 1924.

Runciman, Sir Steven: *The Fall of Constantinople*. Cambridge: Cambridge University Press, 1969.

————: *The Great Church in Captivity*. Cambridge: Cambridge University Press, 1968.

Sahas, D. J.: *John of Damascus on Islam: "The Heresy of the Ishmaelites."* Leiden: E. J. Brill, 1972.

Said, Edward W.: *Orientalism*. New York: Pantheon Books, 1978.

Schwoebel, R. H.: *The Shadow of the Crescent: The Renaissance Image of the Turk, 1453-1517*. Nieukoop: de Graaf, 1967.

Semaan, Khalil I., ed.: *Islam and the Medieval West. Aspects of Inter-cultural Relationships*. Albany: S.U.N.Y. Press, 1980.

Shaw, E. K., and Heywood, C. J.: *English and Continental Views of the Ottoman Empire, 1500-1800*. Los Angeles: University of California, 1972.

Shaw, Stanford J.: *History of the Ottoman Empire and Modern Turkey*. Volume I. *Empire of the Gazis. The Rise and Decline of the Ottoman Empire, 1280-1808*. Cambridge: Cambridge University Press, 1976.

Skilliter, S. A.: "Three Letters From the Ottoman Sultana SaFiye to Queen Elizabeth I," in *Documents from Islamic Chanceries*, Samuel Miklos Stern, ed. Oxford: Oriental Studies, 1965

Skilliter, S. A.: *William Harborne and the Trade with Turkey, 1578-1583. A Documen-*

tary Study of the First Anglo-Ottoman Relations. London: Oxford University Press, 1977.

Sousa, N.: *The Capitulary Regime of Turkey.* Baltimore: The Johns Hopkins University Press, 1933.

Southern, R. W.: *Western Views of Islam in the Middle Ages.* Cambridge: Harvard University Press, 1962.

Stavrianos, L. S., *The Balkans Since 1453.* New York: Holt, Rinehart and Winston, 1961.

Strachan, Michael: *The Life and Adventures of Thomas Coryate.* London: Oxford University Press, 1961.

Stoye, J. W.: *English Travellers Abroad, 1604-1667: Their Influence in English Society and Politics.* New York: Octagan Books, 1968.

Sugar, Peter F.: *Southeastern Europe under Ottoman Rule,* 1354-1804. Seattle: University of Washington Press, 1977.

Taylor, E. R. C.: *Tudor Geography,* 1405-1583. London: Methuen, 1930.

————: *Late Tudor and Early Stuart Geography, 1583-1650.* London: Methuen, 1934.

Thomas, L. V. and Itzkowitz, N.: *A Study of Naima.* New York, New York University Press, 1972.

Tidrick, K.: *Heart-Beguiling Araby.* Cambridge: Cambridge University Press, 1980.

Vaughan, D. M.: *Europe and the Turk: A Pattern of Alliances.* Liverpool: Liverpool University Press, 1954.

Vogt-Göknil, Ulya: *Living Architecture: Ottoman.* New York: Grosset and Dunlap, 1966.

Vryonis, Speros: *Studies on Byzantium, Seljuks, and Ottomans: Reprinted studies.* Malibu, Cal.: Undena Publications, 1981.

Willson, D. H.: *King James VI & I.* New York: Oxford University Press, 1956.

Wilson, C.: *England's Apprenticeship, 16032-1763.* London: Longmans, 1965.

Wittek, Paul: *The Rise of the Ottoman Empire.* London: Royal Asiatic Society of Great Britain and Ireland, 1938.

Wolf, John B.: *The Barbary Coast. Algeria Under the Turks, 1500 to 1830.* New York: W. W. Norton, 1979.

Wood, A. C.: *A History of the Levant Company.* New York: Barnes and Noble, 1935.

Wright, Louis B.: *Middle Class Culture in Elizabethan England.* Ithaca: Cornell University Press, 1958.

————: *Religion and Empire: The Alliance Between Piety and Commerce in English Expansion, 1558-1625.* Chapel Hill: University of North Carolina Press, 1943.

————, and Lamar, V. A., eds.: *Life and Letters in Tudor and Stuart England.* Ithaca: Cornell University Press, 1962.

Wright, W. L.: *Ottoman Statecraft.* Princeton: Princeton University, 1935.

Zinkeisen, G. W.: *Geschichte des Osmanischen Reiches.* Hamburg: F. A. Perthes, 1840-1863.

————: Zwei baierische Türkenbüchlein (1542) und ihr Verfasser." *Bayerische Akademie der Wissenschaften, Philosophisch-Historische Klasse, Sitzungsberichte.* Jahrgang 1959, Heft 4.

————: "Zwei Stambuler Gesamtansichten aus den Jahren 1616 und 1642." *Ibid,* Neue Folge, Heft 5 (1960).

Secondary Sources

Articles

Akdag, Mustafa: "Osmanli Imperatorluğunun Yükselis Devrinde Askeri Düzen." *Tarih Araştirmalari Dergisl*, VI (1965), 139-156.

Anderson, Sonia P.: "Sir Paul Rycaut, F. R. S. (1629-1700): His Family and Writings." *Proceedings of the Huguenot Society of London*, XXX (1970 for 1969), pp. 464-491.

————: "Paul Rycaut and his Journey from Constantinople to Vienna in 1665-1666." *Revue des Études Sud-Est Européenes*, XI (1973), pp. 251-273.

Arnakis, G. G.: "Gregory Palamas Among the Turks and Documents of his Captivity as Historical Sources." *Speculum*, XXXVI (1951), pp. 104-118.

————: "The Greek Church of Constantinople and the Ottoman Empire." *The Journal of Modern History*, XXIV (19529, pp. 235-250.

Babinger, Franz: "Die Aufzeichnungen des Genuesen Iacopo do Promontorio de Campis über den Osmanenstaat um 1475." *Bayerische Akademie der Wissenschaften, Philosophisch-Historische Klasse, Sitzungsberichte*. Jahrgang 1956, Heft 8.

Barkan, Ö. L.: "The Price Revolution of the Sixteenth Century. A Turning Point in the Economic History of the Near East." *International Journal of Middle Eastern Studies*, VI (1973), pp. 3-28.

Baumer, F. L.: "England, the Turk, and the Common Corps of Christendom." *American Historical Review*, October, 1944, pp. 26-49.

Bent, J. T.: "The English in the Levant." *English Historical Review*, V (1890), pp. 654-665.

Biegman, N. H.: "Ragusan Spying for the Ottoman Empire." *Belleten*, XXVII (1963), pp. 237-255.

Brenner, W.: "The Social Basis of English Commercial Expansion, 1550-1650." *Journal of Economic History*, XXXII (1972), pp. 361-392.

Buchanan, Harvey: "Luther and the Turks, 1519-1529." *Archiv für Reformationsgeschichte*, XLVII (1956) pp. 145-160.

Burian, Orhan: "Interest of the English in Turkey as Reflected in the Literature of the Renaissance." *Orients*, V (1952), pp. 209-229.

Burns, R. I.: "Christian-Islamic Confrontations in the West: the Thirteenth-Century Dream of Conversion." *American Historical Review*, Vol. 76 (1971), pp. 1386-1412, 1432-1434.

Cernovodeanu, Paul: "England and the Question of Free Trade in the Black Sea in the Seventeenth Century." *Revue roumaine d'histoire*, VI (1967), pp. 15-22.

——: "The General Condition of English Trade in the Second Half of the Seventeenth Century and the Beginning of the Eighteenth Century." *Revue des études süd-est européens*, V (1967), pp. 447-460.

Collins, Lansing: "Barton's Audience in Istanbul." *History Today*, XXV (1975), pp. 262-270.

Dannenfeldt, K. H.: "The Renaissance Humanists and the Knowledge of Arabic." *Studies in the Renaissance*, II (1955), pp. 96-117.

Forell, G. W.: "Luther and the War against the Turks." *Church History*, XIV (1945), pp. 256-271.

French, D. "A Sixteenth Century English Merchant in Aleppo?" *Anatolian Studies* XXII (1972), pp. 241-247.

Rifa'at A. Abou el-Haj. "Ottoman Diplomacy at Karlowitz". *Journal of the American Oriental Society*, Vol. 87, #4, 1967, pp. 498-512.

P. R. Harris. "An Aleppo Merchant's Letter-Book". *Museum Quarterly*, XXII (1960), pp. 64-69.

Heath. M. J. "Renaissance Scholars and the Origin of the Turks." *Bibliothèque d'Humanisme et Renaissance*, XLI (1979), 453-471.

Hess, Andrew: "The Battle of Lepanto and its Place in Mediterranean History." *Past and Present*, LVII (1972), pp. 53-74.

——: "The Evolution of the Ottoman Seaborne Empire in the Age of Oceanic Discoveries, 1453-1525." *American Historical Review*, LXXV (1970), pp. 1889-1919.

——: "The Ottoman Conquest of Egypt (1517) and the Beginning of the Sixteenth-Century World War." *International Journal of Middle Eastern Studies*, IV (1973), pp. 55-96.

——: "The Moriscos: An Ottoman Fifth Column in Sixteenth-Century Spain." *American Historical Review*, LXXIV (1968), pp. 1-25.

Horniker, A. L. "Anglo-French Rivalry in the Levant from 1583 to 1612." *Journal of Modern History*, XVIII (1946), pp. 289-305.

——: "William Harborne and the Beginning of Anglo-Turkish Diplomatic and Commercial Relations." *Ibid.*, XIV (1942), pp. 289-316.

Hurewitz, J. C.: "Ottoman Diplomacy and the European States System." *Middle East Journal*, XV (1961), pp. 141-152.

Inalcik, Halil: "Bursa and the Commerce of the Levant." *Journal of Economic and Social History of the Orient*, III (1960), pp. 131-147.

——: "Capital Formation in the Ottoman Empire." *Journal of Economic History*, XXIX (1969), pp. 97-140.

——: "Imtiyazat: Ottoman." *Encyclopedia of Islam*, Second ed., vol. IV.

——: "Mehmed the Conqueror (1432-1481) and his Time." *Speculum*, XXXV (1960), pp. 419-427.

——: "Ottoman Methods of Conquest." *Studia Islamica*, Fas. II (1954), pp. 103-129.

——: "Suleiman the Lawgiver and Ottoman Law." *Archivum Ottomanicum*, I, pp. 105-139.

——: "The Economic Situation in Turkey During the Foundation and Rise of the Ottoman Empire." *Belleten*, XV (1956).

Jones, C. M. "The Conventional Saracens of the Songs of geste." *Speculum*, XVII (1942), pp. 201-225.

Jorgensen, P. A.: "Theoretical Views of War in Elizabethan England." *Journal of the History of Ideas,* XII (1952), pp. 469-81.

Kissling, H. J.: "Türkenfurcht and Türkenhoffnung im fünfzehnten und sechszehnten Jahrhunderte." *Südest Forschung,* XXIII (1964), pp. 1-18.

Kortepeter, C. M. "Ottoman Imperial Policy and the Economy of the Black Sea Region in the Sixteenth Century." *Journal of American Oriental Studies* 86/2 (April - June 1966, pp. 86-113.)

Menage, V.: "Some Notes on the *Devşirme.*" *Ibid.,* XXIX (1966), pp. 64-78.

Mumcu, Ahmet: "Kul Sisteminin Ortaya Cikmasi ve Gelismesi," in A. Tietze, *Advanced Turkish Reader.* Bloomington: Indiana University Press, 1973, pp. 115-121.

Munro, D. C. "The Western Attitude Towards Islam During the Period of the Crusades." *Speculum,* VI (1931), pp. 329-341.

Osborn, James M.: "Travel Literature and the Rise of Neo-Hellenism in England." *Bulletin of the New York Public Library,* XXVII (1963), pp. 279-300.

Palmer, J. A. B.: "Fr. Georgia de Hungaria, O. P. and the *Tractatus de moribus conditionibus et nequitia Turcorum.*" *Bulletin of the John Rylands Library,* XXXIV (1951-1952), pp. 44-68.

———: "The Origin of the Janissaries." *Ibid.,* XXXV (1952-1953), pp. 448-482.

Patrides, C. A.: "The Bloody and Cruell Turke: the Background of a Renaissance Commonplace." *Studies in the Renaissance,* X (1963), pp. 126-135.

Pears, Edwin: "The Spanish Armada and the Ottoman Porte." *English Historical Review,* VIII (1893), pp. 439-466.

Podea, I. I.: "Contributions to the Study of Queen Elizabeth's Eastern Policy, 1590-1593." *Mélanges d'histoire générale,* 1938, pp. 423-76.

Rothenburg, G. E.: "Aventinus and the Defence of the Empire Against the Turks." *Studies in the Renaissance,* X (1963), pp. 60-67.

Schoeck, R. J.: "Thomas More's 'Dialogue of Comfort' and the Problem of the Real Grand Turk." *English Miscellany,* XX (1969), pp. 23-37.

Schwoebel, R. H.: "Co-existence, Conversion, and Crusade against the Turks." *Studies in the Renaissance,* XII (1965), pp. 164-187.

———: "Western Spies in the Levant." *History Today,* XIII (1963), pp. 745-766.

Setton, K. M.: "Leo X and the Turks." *Proceedings of the American Philosophical Society,* CXIII (1969), pp. 367-424.

———: "Lutheranism and the Turkish Peril." *Balkan Studies,* III (1962), pp. 133-168.

Shaw, Stanford: "The Aims and Achievements of Ottoman Rule in the Balkans." *Slavic Review,* XXI (1962), pp. 617-622.

Spencer, T. J. B.: "Turks and Trojans in the Renaissance." *Modern Language Review,* XLVII (1952), pp. 330-333.

Stoianovich, T.: "The Conquering Balkan Orthodox Merchant." *Journal of Economic History,* XX (1960), 234-313

Vryonis, Speros jr.: "Isidore Glabas and the Turkish Devshirme." *Speculum,* XXXI (1956), pp. 433-443.

Waggoner, G. R.: "An Elizabethan Attitude toward Peace and War." *Philological Quarterly.* XXXIII (1954) pp. 20-33.

Walsh, J. R.: "Giovanni Tomasso Minadoi's History of the Turco-Persian War of the Reign of Murad III." *International Congress of Orientalists, Proceedings (Trudy).* pp. 448-54 (Moscow, 1960).

William, T. S.: "Some Aspects of the English Trade with the Levant in the Sixteenth Century." *English Historical Review,* LXX (1955), pp. 399-410.

Wilson, K. J.: "More and Holbein: The Imagination of Death." *Sixteenth Century Journal,* VII (1976), 51-118.

Wittek, Paul: "The Turkish Documents in Hakluyt's Voyages." *Bulletin of the Institute of Historical Research,* XIX 57 (1942), pp. 121-139.

———: "Devshirme and Sharia." *Bulletin of the School of Oriental and Asian Studies,* XVII (1955), pp. 271-278.

142

Bibliographies and Reference Works

Bickley, Francis, ed.: *Guide to the Reports of the Royal Commission on Historical Manuscripts, 1870-1914*. Part II. Index of Persons. London: H. M. Stationery Office, 1935.

Birge, J. A.: *A Guide to Turkish Area Study*. Washington: American Council of Learned Societies, 1949.

Cox, C. G.: *A Reference Guide to the Literature of Travel, including Voyages, Geographical Descriptions and Expeditions*. Vol. I. *The Old World*. Seattle: University of Washington Press, 1933.

Dennis, A. L. P.: "Special Collections in American Libraries: The Oriental Collection of Count Paul Riant now in the Library of Harvard University." *Library Journal*, XXVIII (1903), pp. 817-820.

The Encyclopedia of Islam. N. Th. Houtsma, ed. Leiden: E. J. Brill, 1960. New Edition, H. A. R. Gibb, ed. Leiden: E. J. Brill, 1960.

Gollner, Carl: *Turcica. Die europäischen Türckendrucke des XVI. Jahrhunderts*. Berlin: Akademie Verlag, 1961.

Hammer-Purgstall, Joseph von: "Zusammenfassendes Verzeichnis der Europa erschienenen die Osmanische Geschichte betreffenden Werke," in *Geschichte des Osmanischen Reiches*. Pest: Hartleben, 1832, volume X.

Kornkrumpf, Hans-Jurgen: *Osmanische Bibliographie mit besonderer Berücksichtigung der Türkei in Europa*. Leiden: E. J. Brill, 1973.

Meram, A. K.: *Belgelerle Türk-Ingiliz illiskileri tarihi*. Istanbul: Kitapcilik Ticaret Sirketi, 1969.

Moran, Berna: *Türklerle ilgli Ingilizce yayinlar bibliografyasi on besinci yüzyildan on sekizinci yüzyila kadar*. Istanbul: Istanbul Maatbasi, 1964.

Pearson, J. D., ed.: *Index Islamicus. A Collection of Articles on Islamic Subjects in Periodicals and Other Collective Publications*. Cambridge: Cambridge University Press, 1958.

Riant, Paul: *Catalogue de la Bibliothèque de Feu M. Le Comte Riant*, L. de German and L. Polain, eds. Paris: Picard, 1899.

Türk Islam Ansiklopedisi Istanbul, 1943-1967.

Webster, Shirley H. *Voyages and Travels in Greece, The Near East and Adjacent Regions Made Previous to the Year 1802. Being A Part of a larger Catalogue of works on Geography, Cartography, Voyages and Travels in the Gennadius Library in Athens*. Princeton: The American School of Classical Studies at Athens, 1953.

143

Appendix:

Chronological Tables of Ottoman Sultans, to 1730, and English Ambassadors, to 1703

Regnal Years of Ottoman Sultans, 1280-1730
Osman 1280-1324
Orhan Gazi 1324-1359
Murat I 1360-1389
Bayezit I 1389-1402
Mehmet I 1413-1421
Murat II 1421-1451
Mehmet II 1444, 1451-1481
Bayezit II 1481-1512
Selim I 1512-1520
Süleyman I the Magnificent 1520-1566
Selim II 1566-1574
Murat III 1574-1595
Mehmet III 1595-1603
Ahmet I 1603-1617
Mustafa I 1617-1618, 1622-1623
Osman II 1618-1622
Murat IV 1623-1640
Ibrahim 1640-1648
Mehmet IV 1648-1687
Süleyman II 1687-1691
Ahmet II 1691-1695
Mustafa II 1695-1703
Ahmet III 1703-1730

ENGLISH AMBASSADORS AT ISTANBUL, 1583-1702

William Harborne 1583-1588
Edward Barton 1588-1597
Henry Lello 1597-1607
Thomas Glover 1607-1611
Paul Pindar 1611-1619
John Eyre 1619-1621
Thomas Roe 1622-1628
Peter Wyche 1628-1639
Sackville Crowe 1639-1647
Thomas Bendysh 1647-1661
Heneage Finch, Second Earl of Winchelsea 1661-1668
D. Harvey 1668-1672
John Finch 1672-1681
John Chandos 1681-1687
William Trumbull 1687-1691
W. Hussey June-September 1691
William Harbond, 1691-1692
William Paget 1693-1702

Index

148